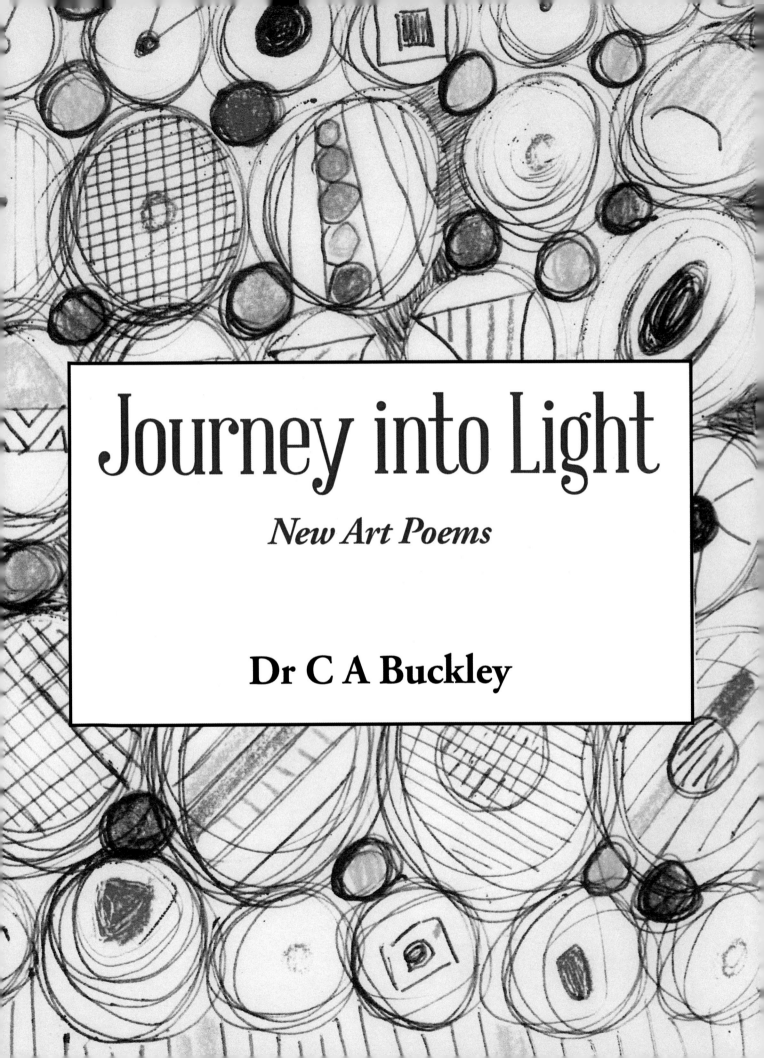

Journey into Light

New Art Poems

Dr C A Buckley

AuthorHouse™ UK
1663 Liberty Drive
Bloomington, IN 47403 USA
www.authorhouse.co.uk
UK TFN: 0800 0148641 (Toll Free inside the UK)
UK Local: 02036 956322 (+44 20 3695 6322 from outside the UK)

This book is printed on acid-free paper.

ISBN: 978-1-6655-9953-5 (sc)
ISBN: 978-1-6655-9952-8 (e)

Print information available on the last page.

Published by AuthorHouse 07/21/2022

author HOUSE®

JOURNEY
into
LIGHT

New Art Poems

By Dr C A Buckley

CONTENTS

The Hiker

Visionary Journeys envisaged by a Youthful Poet:

My Early verses depict imaginary hikes
To various destinations of heart content,
Where darkness dissolves in the bright
Designs and Word Art the poet invents.

As day dawns like a velvet rose
On a birdsong summer morning,
The hiker, a dream-pilgrim poet,
Packs for the road, and sets out.

The air is breathless,
And from its dewy depths
There flows promise.
As the poet hiker tramps
Into the damp shimmering
Mists of a mid-May morning,
His heart is alive and singing;

For a bright dawn is breaking inside,
Like the ruby sun's soft and beaming
Rays, rising to wake a sleeping world,
Daylight streams into his pilgrim soul,
Intimating a summer time of truer art
To come, a wiser freer heart and mind;

Off the road he goes by old paths along
Multi-bloom mist-drenched meadows,
Where soft sticky seeds of May weeds
Cling to his clothes, like winged spirits,
Carrying his soul to visionary heights,
His heart to the arts of truth and light.

"Yes, *today*", he writes, "today
Will be no day of sorrow and sin,
Today I resolve to begin to be;
I'll Journey out of darkness,
Down bright roads of the senses;
Under soft smiling summer skies,
Leaving old dull ways and designs,
I go finally to where my soul's alive.

So though the wet grass clutches
And soaks through to the skin,
With the clammy touch of reality;
Seemingly saying "sink back to banality",
The hiker poet goes on into dawning light,
Following the dreams of his heart and soul
To diamond shores of life and forevermore;
Knowing dull life is the ultimate profanity,
And poetry, like faith, is a glorious insanity.

Thus the lush grass and multi-coloured wild flowers
Of the spring fields he travels, and tapered towers
Of tinted-pink blossoms on overhanging thorn trees,
Image a new unfaltering belief, and their new leaves
His leaving of a waste winter world of weary grief
And pain, to go green highways of heart life again.

II

The sky clears, and a warm sun
Sends clouds of invisible vapour
Into the pale blue mid-May air:
Inside, he enters once more the bright countryside
Of an uncluttered soul: fields of fluffy-clover delight,
Paths of birdsong peace, rivers of plopping trout life;

To his new mind byway fields of wild-flower design
Serve to intimate the various shades of eternal time.
And the blackthorn blessings from heavenly climes,
For it scatters pale pink petals on him and his quest,
As he rests a while to write with newly-revived zest:

"Above me on green sloping hillsides sheep graze,
And the lady furze blazes with fresh orange fires;
And from new-leaved branches in a summer haze,
Male birds with marvellously crafted mating arias,
Lure loveless ladies to nests of lofty tree dalliance;

Shall I cry then, no, I shall laugh,
Walking this heart-warming earth
Where the cuckoo sings, bell clear,
On this cloudless morning of May,
When former grimy times of sad and unmourned sins
Are banished by the shrill spring strings of bird violins,
And the counterpoint base buzzing of busy honey bees";

Leaving composing he goes to meet a farmer and wife,
Driving cattle with hanging udders of milk from a field:
A child walks with them a child like the hiker once was,
A thin pale child, barefoot bare-armed, unworldly wise
With fair hair and clear innocent eyes, portals of a soul
Artless and uninhibited and blue as the overhead skies:

O holy child of the morning fair! The hiker writes again,
Boy with golden curls of the first fire of life in your hair,
Let me be alive like you, fair as I once was, free from care!
Loving life in land of laughing streams and clear fresh air;

Here at the heart of natural humanity, with soul on fire,
Let me feel, freed in mind, the new morning, fully alive:
The warm bright summer morning that's a golden song,
Free from discordant human darkness, war and wrong,
The morning that is this hiker's ideal of peaceful being,
When care is no more; when banished is sombre sorrow;
When the ravaged earth is green once more and whole;
And on rural roads a poet hiker's one with nature's soul".

The Ongoing Journey of the Dream Hiker

"Every day is a journey – he walks off into the mid-May dawn, into the geography of the soul that makes the journey itself a home" – Sam Hamill on Basho's poetic travels.

The people who were secure in bed
The hiker did and did not envy.
It was a suitable morning for setting out again:
Late May, the roadway is already dry as dust;
The roadside rich with grass, weeds, flowers;
The trees leaning over with leaves, fresh born;
These all made him feel in the finest of form.
Only essentials in a light pack on his shoulders,
He goes on golden byways to bold new horizons.

It was then that loneliness struck
The solitary hiker,
The terror of his isolation,
The lot of the outcast;
For he had to face alone
The darkness of the road
To destiny and freedom;
As one grows cold and old,
One feels the terror of not knowing
Where the road is going or will end.

He encamped at evening,
Vermilion with dying fire,
By a stream bubbling over marbled stones,
On spongy spring grass as fresh and green
As was his new-found freer being.
He pitched his tent in an open field,
Where placid cows chewed the cud
And rabbits and many holy birds of the hedges
Peeped out at him, with wildly inquisitive eyes;

Over a fire of sticks
He cooked his meagre meal
And reflected in that green wilderness
On his past plastic technological being,
And his glorious new organic believing.

Under rustling reassuring oak branches,
He lay down under a dome of darkness
And stilled his unholy unquiet eyes
With sleep underneath starry skies;
For the hiker when he slept,
Blended into the green world,
And became a tree, a stone, a flower;
The hiker as he laid the world aside,
Slept well under a tent of owlet eyes,
And woke to an alarm of birds arias,
That spoke to him of emerald fields,
Diamond streams, and far blue hills.

II

You rose with the dawn, hiker:
The singing birds rose with you;
The cock, the cuckoo, the sun;
You began where the day began;
You caught the rose of the dawn
And pinned it to your button hole;
You whistled a gipsy tune to the cars
Of the disappearing moon and stars;

The water is cool, hiker,
As you wash your face in the stream,
As you comb your wetted hair
And touch the water with your nose; as you walk on,
The roadside is a mass of dusty daisies and dandelions,
Their simple designs inspire you to fresh poetic lines;
For as you walk, as the hiker poet, you decide
To make up a rhyme or two to pass the time,
Though it'd pass anyway without any rhymes.

I am the merry hiker
I journey my mortal ways
Into immortal days;
I sing my songs of praise
Into immortal days;
The merry hiker knows
More than any man knows:
The merry hiker goes
Where no one has gone before;
He opens wide the door
To things never seen before;

The world is full of worry
But the hiker's done with care;
The hiker is in no hurry,
He can loll in the country air,
A summer bird of innocence;
In the morning before despair.

This is me as young man:
As I am now old, I laugh
At the optimism with which
My journey of life began.
The Home of Poetry

I remember from my early youth
Five of us with father in one bed;
Three on top and three on bottom,
Legs by heads, and heads by legs.

He'd dream with us each night –
After we had said our prayers
And quenched the candle flame -
Of winning the Sweep one day.

When winter howled around
Our house, and the cold rain
And fierce sleet, and bitter hail
Battered the window panes,

In our old long low farmhouse,
Cramped in a small lower room,
We slept close, storied and warm,
Insulated from all outside storms.

In a jumble of tangled bodies,
We kept each other from loneliness,
Under sheets, woollen blankets,
And spreads mother made for us.

In this small close-knit universe
Of bodily togetherness, we knew
The wild night world raging outside
Could neither destroy nor divide us.

A bonding story my father would
Lull us to sleep with, after prayer,
As we snuggled up to his grey hairs,
Was that we'd go on the roads one day.

We'd live on the highways, like tinkers,
And beg for our food, and be free hearts.
I pondered that grand prospect gleefully,
As each night I drifted into dream lands;

Dad's dream of travelling the roads made me go,
Lifelong, on his free highways of the poetic soul.

II

Yesterday I saw my mother:
Plump and small,
Her glasses hovering
On her nose,
Her tongue clattering
Like bird calls;

Telling poem after poem
To a small wide-eyed boy,
As she was busy baking;
Scattering flour,
And cutting out
The small current cakes I adored.

When the stream stopped,
I fell into a dream,
Where I still am,
Living in the kitchen
Of her poetic heart,
And by the fire
Of her creative being.

For outside of that,
The world always
Seemed raw, rhyme-less,
Time trapped and soiled,
Too hard, cruel and cold;

III

Yesterday I also saw
My pale frail father in old age,
Leaning against a gate
In a Lamanaugh field,
His tall gaunt form
Resting like a tree
In winter;

And he said to me:
"Son, give it all up,
As I did
And be free".

I saw the tree wither
And die before my very eyes;
Yet I knew its branches
Grow green again on high,
Filling the immortal skies;
If, due to Spanish flu, his body was thin and fragile,
He had a wise quiet soul strength and an fine mind.

Sense Worlds of a rural Youth

I can't help having been a child of sense:
I still taste home jam and smell primroses;
I still hate schoolmasters, love my brothers;
I still adore marbles, marshmallow mice
And barefoot feet on grass, snow days,
Christmas holidays, mystic midnight mass;

I can't help having been a child of sense:
I still hear threshing machines humming;
Cocks crowing me awake in the morning;
The quacking of young ducks in the yard
And the fierce hissing of an angry gander;
I still smell the scent of old-roses by our gate,
Honeysuckle in our hedges in the autumn late;
Or musty cow-dung compost by the barn gate.

I can't help having been a child of sense:
I still taste currant bread in a hayfield;
The bitterness of unripe stolen apples;
The blandness of haws, the sourness of sloes;
I still feel cold sheets on my skin at night;
Hear whining of winds in the cold outside,
And feel skin-cosy, safe in bed with siblings;

I can't help having been a child of sense:
I still run barefoot, over sticky-tar summer roads
Or the soft grass of shortcuts across the fields,
Home from school to meals of bacon and cabbage;
I still taste the sweetness of buttered soda bread;
Or smell just-from-the-oven scones mother-made;

I can't regret having been a country child of sense:
I still hear crickets chirping in the evening;
The clamour of distant cranes;
The noisiness of crows in tall trees near the stall
As I milk the cows, their udders slimy to touch,
And sloppy-wet with milk under my hands;
I still see the fatness of ticks swelled with cows' blood
I pull from their hides and squelch to pulp with stones;

I can't regret having been a country child of sense:
I can still see the stark yellowness of after-birth cow milk;
The blueness of thistles, the whiteness of hoar-frost fields;
I still feel under bare feet fluffy clover and spongy grass;
I still feel pleasure in picking plump autumn mushrooms,
Fawn underneath, but pure black when fried in butter;

I can't help having been a child of sense:
I still hear the persistent splutter of an engine
As my older brother fixed his first motor bike,
His hands smeared with black slimy motor grease;

I can't help having been a child of sense in rural innocence;
Youth today adore shiny tech machines and computer toys;
So do I; yet I crave soft things to keep my inner child alive.
Like a child with a grubby comforter, shunning costly toys.

Bird Candles flying into light

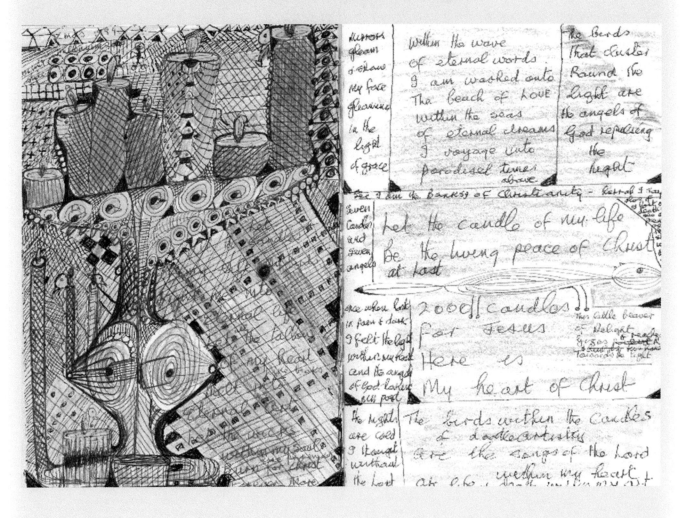

When the Flesh was Young

In the flesh when we were young
All of life was a carefree song:
Swimming, games, wrestling;
Running, jumping, joy-riding;
Camping, hiking, orchard raiding;
Rolling down the Dane's grassy glen
With shrieking siblings and friends. Singing:
"God be with the days when we were young
And rolling down the glens for fun".

Climbing high mountains:
In the fields, in the forests;
By the springs, by the rivers;
On the roads, by a blue sea;
Barefoot, sunburnt and free.

Skipping on sand:
The waves rolling over us;
The surf washing us;
Drying with towels,
Our wet skin, on warm sand;

The climbing of rocks;
Picking of periwinkles;
The plucking of sea weed;
The gathering of curved coloured shells
That echoed sea waves held to our ears;

The sheltering from the rain
Under dripping trees:
Under bushes, under umbrellas;
The sweet scent of the earth
After a sudden summer shower;

The trekking over bogs, over heather:
The lying on moss in sunny weather;
The touch of warm lips against lips;
Of hand against tender hand beneath
Spring-blossom petal-snowing trees;

The grand feeling for hours
Of the sun on our bronze bodies;
The gentle brushing of the soft
Summer winds though our hair;
The setting of snares by rabbit lairs.

Such were our airy beings,
Like swallows on the wing,
Free children, wild and running,
Enjoying sunlit summers of fun,
In the flesh when we were young.

Aged Care

Now aged care leads me into ways
I would not go; up hills of darkness,
Through dusky valleys of despair;
There the oncoming snow at first
Falls in tears; there's often a starkness
About my situation, as wolves gather
In packs about the doors of my soul,
A dingy cabin among winter woods;

Woods of the heart: broods of ravens,
Dark, glossy and intense, view
Me with ravenous eyes; and eagles
Soar above, their piercing cries
Penetrating my dying body, feeding
On eroding cells in my fading brain;

At night petulant pigeons like sighs
Mock my wakefulness; their hollow
Mournful cries intimate my demise.

Will there be a tomorrow for me
In this locked lonesome cabin of age?
For it seems that sly foxes padding
Through the tangled undergrowth,
Carry the very bodies of my dreams;
Senseless white rabbits, dripping death,
Gripped in time's rabid indifferent teeth?

Yet, thoughtfully, in art and in faith,
I'd wriggle out of the teeth of death.

Vision, a Return to Poetry

Suddenly I saw the light:
One night all alone,
And seemingly having lost
All love of life and delight.
I saw a great glowing light,
And within its heart
I saw an angel of mirth,
A smiling laughing spirit
From the land of love
And insight and truth.
And he said to me, not out laud
But deep in my heart,
Cheer up the world God made
Is not dark and cold,
But glowing with colour,
Variety, and splendour untold.
It was October 2021:
And I looked out my window
At my garden with its flowers,
And rosy apples, plums and pears;
And trees turning red and gold,
And falling leaves like inner fires.
And I said should I not see
The beauty all around and within me?
For the world we live in,
Is the world we create of good or ill,
Of gloom or joy, of bad or good will.
And suddenly I heard a bird singing,
And it was the song of my lost delight,
Bringing poetry back as warm dawn light,
After the dark and damp of a dreary night.

Prayer

Grace of breath is given to me
Even in this clear afternoon
Beside the irate sea:
"A salad of lilies in the bud",
From towers moon white,
Down the stair-stepped air,
Smiles under roses falling;
I let the summer trees and water
Enter the ajar soul.

The small birds that skirt
The foam of an inward winter
Tell again the dream was gazing,
Innocent, at the lost golden sand
And the swirling diamond water;

That dream is now
The snowy gloss of pearls;
The heart's profit of painless grace,
And the mind's all-seeing plenty;

If something of me
Is not yet complete -
Afloat on a motion
That divides and breaks -
May it one day be mastered into art,
Caught up in a crushing net of peace.

The Cowslip

Today I saw a meadowland cowslip
In my border flower bed, hanging
Its three-ringlet yellow-haired head.
And I remembered the raw wonder
Of finding it a year ago in golden bloom
On my lawn, amazed the sit-on mower
Hadn't beheaded the rare fragile flower.
And I had so carefully dug it up, in order
To plant it tenderly in my border instead,
Like a smiling child I was putting to bed.

Now a year later, I find it flowering
In the power of late spring sunshine.
It had survived as I had planned,
For if it had remained in the fields
It would long since have been torn
To shreds, for now they cut fields
To the bone, and all the little tender
Sleeping wild flowers, like my cowslip,
End up crushed in brackish silage bales.
But I had, in a small way, done my level best
To restore the cowslip to its natural clay nest,
Until a new world's created, natural, unspoiled,
When the cowslip, the countryside's shy child,
A secret gem, flourishes once more in the wild;

And I cried, cowslip of the heart,
Pet of our country's free field art,
Let me take your part in today's tech earth!
The cowslip held up its pale-gold-nodding
Little heads and said, "Hey! I'm oh so glad
You took me and put me in your warm bed".
"Indeed cowslip of farmland finery", I replied,
"I wish you were my yellow-haired little wife,
And you'd a home, as of old, free from strife,
In national pastures that nurtured wild life".

Back to Boherbue

In merry yet painful memory,
Discovering the cowslip
Made my mind wander
Down the road of my youth,
To a cabin of rich poverty.
Where we were reared like wild flowers
In Lamanaugh's wet rushy meadowlands.

It was there I first saw truth
Near Boherbue, yellow road
To obscurity and divinity.
There I both felt the sorrows of life,
And knew the God of living simply.

There I bore Lamanaugh Cross
On my shoulders many a day,
On my Golgotha way to school.
Where under the rule of a harsh master,
Pontius Pilate Murphy I named him,
My hands were mashed red every day;
He taught catechism, Pontius Pilate Murphy,
But he never learned the meaning of mercy.

The while, despite it all, I let another
Master my mind, and bear the grudge
Until the pain was lost in memory.
Happily, we mostly remember only good things:
Nothing's perfect, I let grudges fade with youth.

I let the best live on in more life-giving memory:
Thus I can still remember my gentle saintly aunt
In an open trap, after mass in Herlihy's shop yard,
Handing out chocolate bars to four happy children.

Her loving kindness healed all the scars of poverty
School tyranny, and drudgery in a moment, raising
Our hearts into a heaven of happy chewing mouths.

Ongoing Journeys of the Dream Hiker

"The sun and moon are eternal travellers" - Basho

I felt like I had to go on the road once more;
Though it was in the dark depths of winter,
With ice like glass glistening on tinsel grass,
And my thatch now as grey as the hoar frost.

I walked out down winding waste ways,
With icy pools mirroring cloudy dreams;
As we proceed, my soul and I, ignoring hail
And the occasional blown sweep of sleet,
We meet fellow travellers on the road:
Some carrying nothing,
Others with loads on their backs;
Some walking swiftly and confidently;
Some trudging along
Backs bent, eyes downcast;
We walk mile after mile
Through village and town;
Uphill and downhill into the heart
Of our great wild wet winter isle.

We meet travellers
By the roadside:
With their rough shelters,
Smouldering fires,
And ragged rusty-headed children;
Old ladies begging,
Half-hidden in shawls,
And strong hefty men driving piebald ponies.
Multi-coloured rags scattered around.

The damp smouldering
Smell of the camp;
The strange wild gaiety
Of the children of the open air;
The rough culture
Of their unsophisticated sport -
Now relegated to urban jungles -
Recalled my own poor youth
On a small farm in north Cork;

Are we still such free children
Of nature's wild domain?
Or are we bound by plastic times?
Are we caged in city box-homes?
Does urban life fail to keep us wild?
Simple citizens of a green Irish soil?

We passed towns before long:
Busy country market towns,
With their rows of pubs,
And gossip and curiosity;
Timeless unhurried towns
Where my soul and I stop to drink and talk
In pubs smelling of porter and stale smoke;

We sit by an old farmer in the corner recreating
With his son, in tattered clothes and wellingtons,
Wearing the usual caps and nursing pints of plain;

A townee perched importantly up at the bar
Was conversing with an aproned proprieter
About local affairs and the latest scandals;
The owner was polishing glasses languidly;
The old farmer and son, worried by storms of sleet,
Left their drinks to hurry home to house the sheep.

Are you too going further than this kip,
The proprietor said to me with a wink:
Ah yes, I replied, much further;
Through floods and through fields;
Slipping on mud;
Sliding down banks;
Sailing on swollen rivers;
Riding and hiking and cycling;
Singing or weeping;
Eating and sleeping;
Loving and hating;
Yet always knowing the one who waits
And where home is;

No, the heart is not at rest
Nor is the mind free from fear;
We've known much anxiety;
We've shed many a tear; we've watched the sad passing
Of many misspent years and many a misguided passion;

Yes, we did sometimes
Grow tired of the journey,
We, being my soul and I,
Of the rain and the dark
And the pain of lifting aching feet;
Of the awesome silence
Of our own touchless individuality;
And the uncertainty of life's destiny.

Yes, we reached out for a hand to hold
When the cold invaded our bones
And merciless monotony oppressed
The novelty seeking
Of the insatiable heart;
But there was not always someone there;

Someone to care and comfort;
But we learned to endure
The kicks; the doors slammed in our faces;
The unkind words; the hard voices,
And to be grateful when an old woman
In a lonely cottage, in some wild domain,
Invited us to sit down close by the fire,
And drink a cup of tea or a hot whiskey;

Or when a farmer,
With a generous homely wife,
And a fine batch of children,
Invited us to rest awhile
And taste some humble hospitality;
Which was once our land's speciality.

Some desired money from us,
But we had none,
For we found wealth a burden on the way,
A false trail to hell, leading us astray;
So we brought with us but our frailty,
And the stainless gold we'd one day be.

The old man laughed again, as he died,
How idealistic I am to the end, he cried;
But I was right, we must defy life's darkness,
We must fill with light all worldly emptiness.

The Buckley Children

Under Clara mountain,
By Tubrid's fountain,
Where holy hermits
Healed souls of yore,
I wander gaily,
And ponder gravely,
On all the beauties
Of a Duhallow home.

In green-glenned Cullen,
Where the busy heron,
Pluck trout like herring
From the Araglen,
My forefather's history,
On gravestones misty,
I wipe and read,
By Latiernan's well.

And then I motor,
To windswept Boher,
Twixt Allow bounded
And the Araglen,
Where hazy sunshine
Show the Buckley children,
By the gracious hamlet
Where their lives began.

Boherbue Melancholy

When I was young,
In the long cold nights
I was sung to,
By the wind whining
Round the lower room
Of our cot in North Cork;

In that refuge in Boherbue
I heard the crying of each tree
As a soul in pain;
And each night, after my mother
Quenched the light of the oil lamp
And the sleet beat against my pane,
I heard the wailing of the icy rain
As the Banshee calling,
From the swimming bogs
Of Lamanaugh and Liseenafeelah.

Calling me, as a child of melancholy,
To the edge of the frothy Araglen,
To leap in, alone in the dark, and die;

Now I am no longer a boy
And in the Lord's land of Palestine
I wish but to live and survive
In the joy of God's warmer clime;

Yet to be really alive and free,
Despite its lingering melancholy,
I always go back to Boherbue.

Boyhood Days in Old Duhallow

Duhallow days taught us boys how to be,
The old man said, in nostalgic revelry:
Those were days of youthful joy,
Playing like swallows on the wing all day;
Wading into the Araglen stream, we angled
With mum's jam-jars for minnows in the shallows;
Our day was rural-child play, bronze barefoot boys
Roving muddy roads and fields, enjoying nature's toys.

"Twas the worst and best of times": poor travellers,
Rich as angels, we wore nature's wild wings,
Not bothering about tattered clothes, dirty faces,
Or uncombed dishevelled hair; in short pants
Made from flour bags, play clothes, we passed
Summer days saving hay, or footing black turf sods
In wind-swept bogs, drinking sweet creamy flasks of "tay",
With buttered soda bread Ma brought in neat reed baskets,
As we watched Daddy slean the black sods onto soft banks
Of deep red heather, by blown bog cotton, biting midges
And frogs croaking deep in last-years dug-out bog holes.

After school in fields of spring we went wild,
Rabbit hunting and birds nesting:
Loving the dotted sky-blue blackbird eggs
And spotted brown ones of the speckled song thrush;
Both nestled in plush mansions
Of down-lined cosiness, in recesses of thorn trees,
Or hidden deep in scratchy golden furze;
Best was the moss football of the robin red breast's
Neat nest with just enough of an opening in its side
For her tender body to wriggle in and rest on her eggs;
We marvelled when these birthed tiny naked babies
With gaping begging beaks, forever hungry it seems.

We fished for fat flashing rainbow trout,
Bright fish like a fairground, green
Grey and red scales roaming a dashing
Rushing river like our young dreams;
Or hiding in dark pools deep as our desires.

We ate them in golden evenings
Before bellows-blown turf fires,
As we listened spell bound to elders' stories
Of fairies that dwelt in our high Fort Field,
Where they said wee-bodied men
And women came out nightly to dance and sing merrily.
As we did occasionally, also knocking sparks off the floor
In set dances all night long after Station rituals
Were over, and Connors from up-the road
Played on a weather-beaten accordion
Foot-tapping fairy-taught tunes wondrous
As those warm summer days were long.

A Home of Poetry

At night my dad recited poems of our cousin
Ned Buckley, the noted bard of Knocknagree:
Lines about an old-style wake enthralled me:
"They took snuff as they rose from their knees
From the one who was there to attend
And said as they started to sneeze,
He wasn't long going in the end".
My mother recited long recitations of other country lore:
Such as militant verses from the land war:
"We'll soon tyrannise that JP in Stake Hill";
"Why walk thru our fields in gloves,
Stake Hill landlord agent nobody loves?
Or songs of Rory the Bold Raparee:
"Up from his couch of green heather
He leaped to the dawning of day
And called on his comrades to follow
As they mounted their steeds and away"
Or *"the dawn was breaking bright and fair*
And a lark sang in the sky,
As a maiden bound her golden hair,
With a bright glance in her eye.
For who beyond the gay green woods
Awaited her with joy?
Who but her gallant Reneree
On the mountain of Pomeroy;
An outlawed man in a land forlorn
He scorned to turn and fly, but he kept
The flag of Ireland free upon the mountain high;
Or *"who can tell where Crowley*
Fell to set old Ireland free –
A Cork rebel she loved Irish nationalist romance;

Or poems from greatest poets of the past,
Long extracts from Sir Walter Scott:
"*The stag at eve had drunk his fill*
Where danced the moon on Monan's Rill…";
Or Oliver Goldsmith's wise words –
"*Ill fares the land to hastening ills a prey,*
Where wealth accumulates and men decay"-
A criticism she applied to our day;
As she did the bard's verse –
"*The evil that men do live after them but the good*
Is often interred with their bones".
Such lines as mantras long mesmerised my mind.

Her reciting was interspersed with weeping
When her verses stirred our heart strings:
As in "An Arab's Farewell to his Steed":
"*Who said that I hath given thee up?*
Who said that I hath sold?
Tis false, tis false, my Arab steed,
I'll fling them back their gold" – it was his soul –
Do some in our land sell their souls today for EU gold?"

Her saddest poem was the "*The Wreck of the Hesperus*":
"*It was the schooner Hesperus*
That sailed the winter sea,
The skipper brought his little daughter,
To bear him company"
Molly's tears came copiously when the death
Of the little girl in the chill sea she recounted:
"*God save us all from a fate like this*
On the reef of Norman's woe".
From this great literary mother I also learned
Faith, she defined it as doing the will of God;
"*I sat in the school of sorrow,*

The master was standing there,
He said son thou must learn thy lesson,
And say thy will be done";
Her word art not only enthralled me but told me
That to be a poet one had to have a tender heart;
Her poems were so wise, well-chosen and so fine
I longed to be a poet and write like memorable lines.

I interrupted the old man, saying in schools now
They educate everything except key aspects of life,
Our feelings, our sensibility and a soul nurturing
For a glorious eternity. The best educators of man
Are art, nature and the deep wisdom of the divinity:
Like great all civilizations our nation once knew
That we needed religious bases to be truly human.
Not that I am seeking to return to a poorer past,
I only assert that we have to have inner riches that last.
For, as Dad said, if our nurturing heritage is faithless,
Our nation's future is bleak, it's certain to be soulless.

The old man went on: sure spiritual nurture
Wasn't neglected in those old Duhallow days:
Sundays we went excited in horse and trap
To Sunday mass, rugs covering us in the cold,
And our saintly aunt hugged us on her lap.
On reaching the church onto the galleries
To look down on the obscure mystic deliveries
Of the latin-chanting priest. We were envious
Of the wine he drank, but knew in awed silence,
It wasn't just wine, but the very person of Christ.
We enjoyed sticky toffee and orangeade afterwards
In Herlihy's shop's trap yard, and then off home
To breakfast on sausages, rashers and eggs,
Heartedly appreciated after the communion fast;

Enjoyed with sweet milky tea and sultana scones
Mother had baked in our black cake oven,
Covered with red coals and cooked slowly in
An open turf fire, fare fit for angels in heaven.

That's gone now like heavy snowfalls of my birth year;
One can't turn back the clock, the old man said with a tear;
Now my sadder lot is to be perched over a computer
And tied to plastic tech displays and ways. I adore the toys
Of modern progress, yet sometimes long for the salad days,
When we were special as blackbirds wooing
Lustily in wet and windy Boherbue weather.
For I remember another dictum of my father,
If we've no past, sure we've no future either.

At this I interrupted the old man's nostalgia trip
With a comment: *That was your age,*
Now it seems as remote as rambling houses
And birds singing on holm oak branches;
Children today spend their time texting
On mobile phones or playing tech war games,
And that's the way they must be in order
To be part of today's modern urban society;
And obey a box mother, as my nephew told me:
"Uncle, you must see we were reared by the TV".
If I ask them anything I know what they're
Going to say according to the conditioning media.
Shaped by bland imported TV-media ideology,
Real original thinking is almost an impossibility.
Yet at least, due to that, they love the environment
And would restore the isle's original emerald tint.

Yet nowadays is nature deranged into a righteous
And much too abstract ideology of climate change?
Is urging us to make green the country again

Grandiose talk in self-gratifying paper conferences?
Urban conservationists exalt nature,
But seldom really immerse their white office hands
And heads in the real humble clay,
From which they came and will return to one day.
Shouldn't we strive now also for a life one with nature
Like you lived as a country boy?
As I try to live today in Ballyduff, in natural delight
And soul-filled seaside salad days.
The bard's question shouldn't be "to be or not to be",
But **how** to **be** naturally happy in any age or country.

Snow Birthday

1947 year of the snow

A year after I was born came the year of the snow, 1947 — maybe that is why snow still has a sort of spiritual intensity for me. What we remember early lodges like a pearl in our brains, in our nourished from the forefront of memory. That snow they say so blocked the windows of the low house that when they woke in the morning it still seemed night, no light but cold blowing snow entered the door when they opened it. It better blew from the east. My father feet-forced themselves through it with the help of a spade to the cowhouse where the cow huddled together had to be hayed & cleaned out from & watered each day, regardless of snow as winter or blowing hail. The pail was frozen for the water & had to be thawed after the fire was stoked from the kindled coals under

fill up the golden little

Bog Men, Olden Kin

In dreams I see my dead kin cutting turf on a bog
In Barna, old withered men of a lost culture,
The few men left in a dying country, once
A land of dreams. Men with faces weathered
As the stones of their fields, with characters
As ageless and powerful as the waste moors.
They worked on, men accustomed from their youth
To toil and poverty, to struggling with infertile
Soil, men with souls as rugged as the mountains
They stood under, men of custom and character.

Yet men of decay, the last of a dying breed,
Slowly passing away, the last of the poor
Cultured farmers of the Ireland of my youth.
There they sit at lunch time on a brown bank
Eating cake bread, drinking tea, reprising
Stories, the remnant of an impressive race,
Close to the soil, and so both brutal and wise.
For recognising the dust from which we came,
Is vital for our voyage to an immortal name.

These are burned into my memory forever more,
Men and women as hoary and heavy and old,
As the hard wet country they were one with,
And the cold agelessness of the earth
They toiled in and tilled in ancient pride,
And died quietly by their own plain turf fireside.

The Old Man recalls the Rambling Houses

Enough of postmodernist philosophy
I said to the old dead man one day,
After we'd drunk our fill
Of Middleton malt that made us jolly:
Sing me a lively song,
That will melt all our troubles away
And take us back momentarily to days long gone
When you lived among merriest women and men,
Who met nightly in rambling houses in the glen community;
It was rural entertainment, there was no TV or radio then.

Bedad I'll tell you about them, he said, and gladly:
Out with it then I said; and this is the song to which
Our lively whiskey partying led. Laughing
I imagined him now singing such songs on high,
Angels and Peter coming to hear the web of words,
And join in the lively dances strumming harp chords:
I'll sing to you of the family
That gathered in the glen:
There was Micky Mack
And Thady Pat,
And the sisters Kat and Nell,
Who battered the floors,
When the night was old,
With lively reels and jigs,
And joyous set-dance lore
From ceilidhs at the crossroads.

Out with the stout,
Patie Pad would shout,
And the Dane the keg rolled out:
And Mick the Doll,

And his sister Moll,
Would pass the bowl around.
Then Mick Muldoon,
From the top of Coom,
Would sing of the Tailor Bawn,
And tell of the night,
Of the tinkers fight,
In the time of the harvest moon.

Then Manio and Con the Crow,
And the feisty Foxer Lane,
Would call for tae,
And currant bread,
And a jorum of Jer's poiteen,
Made in a back room shebeen.

At this I tried to stop the old man,
But suddenly he was off again:
Sing to me of the family
That gathered in the glen:
There was Tim the tailor
And his daughter Maura,
And the tinkers Bod and Dod,
And close to the fire
Sat the maestro Maguire,
Fiddling away like mad.

Then Mikey Tom,
Called for a song,
To set the tables rattling,
And sweetly sang his daughter Kathleen
The Wind that shakes the barley,
Tom sang *The Bold Thady Quill*,
And his girl sang *Ned of the Hill*;
Ah, they were treasures surely!

Here I tried to intervene again,
But the roused old man
Had the reins in his hands,
And began the refrain again:

Sing to me of the family Magee
That gathered in the glen:
There was Hanny the horse,
And the hearse o'Flynn,
And Jack Thade John's young son.
There was Paddy the Priest,
And the Cap O Keefe,
And the thatcher Davoo Con;
And Jule the Lao,
And Jimmy the Lady,
(so called because he'd seven daughters),
And the lodger Paddy Den.
There was Murphy the Man,
And his daughter Han,
And Maggie at the top of the hill.

There was old Jack Bat,
Of the yellow bacon,
And the badger Flor O'Brien;
And the boar McNee,
And the weaver Dan,
And the Bard of Knocknagree.
And Kelly the seanachie,
Who told old tales with glee,
While Biddy served cakes and tea,
And said with pleasure,
As the dancers got ready,
"Round the house and mind the dresser".

At this I said stop!
We'll sing another time,
Of your youth among men,
Of character and learning,
Who lived by the Dane's glen.

The memories of distinguished men
And women too, like Mary Drew of the Co-op,
The shop, who'll never come again, I said sighing,
Ah, he said, the world was young and simple then,
But time moves on for better or worse, that's fine!
We should be thankful that nothing is set in stone,
For the poverty or ignorance of my era's also gone,
With its slavish farm work and rare snatches of fun.

Like the glitter of morning dew, the nature of human life
Is that it must always be new, yet our modern country,
In my view, have abandoned, for a banal TV superficiality,
Much of a great heritage of originality and authenticity.
If we erode the core of the Irish soul we're rootless plants
Blown hither and thither by storms of imported
Shifting cultural weather, third class citizens
Of cultural heritages of other lands we should enrich.
Let's see sense, that a rich ancestral legacy
Can be retained beside modern progress.
I said, you want the best of past and present rolled into one;
And why not, he cried, are you sure that it can't be done?

Wings out of Darkness

The old man was enamoured with certain spiritual books
Like the Egyptian Book of the Dead. He thought modern Man was a fool, he nurtures
everything unimportant and Passing except his immortal soul. All great civilizations
Had Faiths to nourish souls both for here and eternity.
So why do moderns fail to aid the church in its essential role,
To satisfy a spiritual hunger in today's malnourished souls?

For there is a darkness within us all, since the fall,
My mentor since I was a child, my old man, observed.
It needs to be dispelled by virtue, and built
By church faith and worship, lest darkness becomes
Our eternal legacy and we're left to roam a cold
Soulless world alone here and lost on forever shores.
For every man's spiritual journey is gradual going
Out of darkness into a dawning brightness of being,
So when he dies he rises to heights of light undying.

II

But beware the cold!
The old man said,
The land of the living dead!
Beware the foul fold
Where the dark lord dwells!
Cast off his chains and wear
The wings of the blest instead.

Beware the cold!
The old man said,
The abode of dead souls,
Where the shore of fire,
Turns to icy ashes the future glory
For which we were designed.

All this I've learned, the old man said,
From perusing *The Book of the Dead*
And pondering on the *Sea of Reeds*.
There I saw myself forever laughing,
In the place where good men go;
All around were glowing verdant valleys,
And mountains capped with pearly snow,
And ageless magnificent mansions of the Word,
Paradises of joy, good people's everlasting reward.

The Book of the Dead

The Book of the Dead, the old man said,
Tells of our journey after death
To the paradise of *The Sea of Reeds;*
And the spiritual devices we need,
To take us past all the demons
That would seize and drag to darkness
Our souls as we passed.
It is journey's end;
Where we finally cash in
The accumulated earthly cheques
Of our virtue, practised faith and worship,
And those amassed and enduring treasures
Of good deeds stored down through the years.

Thus, like the bible,
The book tells us how to attain
An everlasting soul ease,
By means of the light
We built within
While on earth's premises.
For us Christians
It's built by means of the church,
The inner riches in the spirit beyond death
Provided by worship and a communal faith.
For the failure of *The Book of the Dead* creed
Was it provided but for the rich and rulers needs,
Claiming riches are needed to have in eternity.
This is unlike Christ's eternal way which is for all,
For a deeper life here and for forevermore,
Especially for the poor, the needy, and the oppressed,
Who're compensated fully for their suffering on earth.
Ah, old man I said, you're over-sermonising, be cool!

OK, he said, May I just re-affirm the church's role?
As we go into a great beyond, we're thus not alone,
We're beyond the clutching claws of the evil demons
Of eternal death, their claws won't finally haul us in,
If our souls are kept alive in a faith family from birth,
Free of demonic unbelief or spiritual aridity on earth.

a spark of light
from out of
    my heart
startled the devils
    steady bark
By which he ferried
    soul on soul
To dark & death
    forever more

It was the spark
    of the Saving
        Lord
& the wondrous
        beauty
of the WORD

Feeling God

We do not think out God, like a puzzle,
We can only feel God, deep down,
Where everything is understood;
That early in life I realised, listening
To the wisdom the old man supplied.

We feel God
In every good within us,
In every starry sky that stuns us,
In every clown that makes us laugh.

We feel God
In every dawn that dazzles us,
In every dog
That licks our face,
In the soft touching warmth
Of every true lover's embrace.
For womanly and manly beauty,
Is part of the beauty of the divinity.

We feel God
In every good drink
Which slakes our thirst,
In every Christmas cheer
That warms our hearts,
In every grand display
Of the finest dazzling arts.

We feel God
In the forests and in the flowers:
In the torrents
And in the waterfalls,
And in the singing birds
Of the morning of all our dreams.

But most of all we, my soul and I,
Feel the loving reality
And the real closeness of God
In our prayers, and especially
In communion in the church community;
The consummate food of the faithful's unity.

We who feel free
In Christ delight
Know what it is like
To be sick
To suffer
To face the night
And not be afraid
We who braid
A garment of God's grace
Know
It will protect us
Though the storm rage
And the cold assails
We who shape
A helmet of faith
A belt of hope
And shoes of charity
Know that we are allfitted
to go
Into the lowest hell
Of our own
He art to sweep it clean
We who stand
In Gods presence day & night
Thank him every day
with ever flowing heart
That we are allowed to do Po

Sonnet at Cullen's Holy Well

Old, I revisit Cullen's well; a boy I loved the holy ground;
Now I climb its stile to pray by its new concrete surround.
As my reflection mingles with shining pennies cast down,
I kneel on flowers by which pilgrims pave the holy mound.

The water's clear and cool. In shimmering summer silence
Long-legged insects waltz across its clear rink-like surface;
I dip fingers in an up-bubbling crystal. Unused to violence,
The spirits flee to Latiernan, a saint of pure water silence.

Like him I delve within, questing for springs of perfection;
As clouds wander in the heavenly blue rippling reflections,
Strong desires well up in me for a world free of corruption.

From the shining spring I splash icy freshness on my face.
I drink its cool wholeness. As old rural simplicity replaces
City complexity my soul's filled at a spring of crystal grace.

Bringing the Cows Home at first Light

My tall frail father was gentle
When he called me in the morning,
Just when Lamanaugh was dawning
Over Sheehan's high green lawn;
He called me to bring the cows
To be milked from the after-grass
In a few fields further up the hill;
And I rose, rubbing sleep
From my eyes, not wholly
Relishing the prospect of
Of going into the cold misty
November frosts that hung over
The less soggy pasture opposite Mikey Tom's house,
A ring-fort field where on after-grass cattle browsed.

I walked there chilled to the bone
Past Lamanaugh cross, uphill
To where the cows waited
At the gate, ready to come home
And be relieved of the weight of milk,
Sometimes oozing from their swollen paps,
If at times I was late bringing them home.
In the stalls they stood like sentinels
As I milked each slowly by hand,
Each stroke chiming in the pail
And churning like the golden butter
We made from their creamy sacrifice.

I have long left our wet rush-filled land;
We were all eager to retire
From its poverty and hard toil;
So that wild way of life is gone:

The cattle, the fields, the fog,
The milking by hand
And the making and salting
Of butter in shiny steel pans;

All things and man ever move on;
That's all gone to time and history;
And so is my frail father.
Yet I still hear him calling me
From his Cullen home of clay,
Calling in a gentle fatherly way:
"Get up my son, it is the dawn
Of another busy day on the farm";

Since, in my heart love of the land lingers on;
I am, and I'm proud to be, a poor farmer's son.

Suppers of Light

Be set once more in imagination
The simple suppers of home,
The old man said, in a reflective tone:
Irish soda bread,
Crossed and buttered
Upon the bread board
Of heaven; lumps
Of steaming lamb
In an Irish stew;
Glasses of golden
Irish mountain dew.

Be set at night time,
The gentle lights of my youth:
Let sods of oil-soaked turf
Light up my bedroom;
Let the smoke be sweet incense,
And let soft lights of oil lamps
Burn my present pettiness away;

Be set as in youth the pleasure of poetry:
Let them set yellow wax candles
About my musing mind; let them put
These candles in silver candlesticks;
To light me up like wine in fine Waterford crystal glasses,
In an intimate dining room of fine dazzling inspirations;
Let them say a Boherbue Buckley boy wrote untold poems,
Free and fanciful as angels singing in heaven's high homes.

Later, as after religious life and ordination,
Be set out the rich rituals of a priestly vocation:
If they pick out my eyes like cocktail olives,

Let them see behind the irises the stained glass
Windows of my inner sacristy, where stands
The small chapel of my frail ordained ministry;
Thereby let them feast on the finest food of fraternity,
Christ's cup of divine wine, clear pathway to eternity.

As He Sees Modern Disorders the Old Man deplores all Man-made Borders

I with fearful thread, walk the deck my captain lies, fallen, cold and dead- Whitman

As borders are set up
Against the suffering refugees,
Said the old man (my mentor and muse, since dead),
I assert that there are no borders in real humanity,
Or in the cosmic village of the universe's divinity.
(*I agreed, hard borders are a heretical profanity!*):

It's man who creates borders:
Walls to keep people out;
Or keep people in;
Or keep people down;
Or deny people being.

There are no borders in humanity
Or in the universe of the divinity;
It is small man who creates borders:
Borders in our minds;
Walls in our hearts;
Barbed wire around our souls;

There are no borders in humanity
Or in the nation of the divinity;
It is small man who creates borders:
Fences around our gold;
Fetters around our loves;
Chains around our imaginations;
Ropes around our hopes;

There are no borders in humanity,
Or in the universe of the divinity;
Small people create borders:
Electronic gates around our homes;
Guards around our aspirations;
Soldiers around our inspirations;
Ramparts around our dreams;
Barbed wire around our beliefs,
(*No publishing for my "religious" poetry?*).

There are no borders in humanity,
Or in the universe of the lord;
It is fallen man or woman who creates borders:
Nets around our thoughts;
Patches over our eyes;
Muffs around our ears;
Lest in seeing we believe,
And on hearing the Truth
Our souls come into the light.

There are no borders in humanity,
Or in the universe of the divinity;
It is small men or women who creates borders:
Borders of gulag ideological insanity;
Borders of profanity;
Borders of hypocrisy;
Borders of corruptibility;
Borders of misogyny;
Borders of racial exclusivity;
Borders that narrow life to arrogant abstract science;
Notional nation borders that spawn endless violence;

II

Soon there will be no need
For borders anymore,
As things fall apart
And the cold darkness
Becomes the only humanity
We can infold.

As the apocalypse descends
On a borderless world,
In the form of rising seas,
There will be no more use
For borders of power and control;
With the waves we may see an end
To all the borders of the evil one?
Cleansing us back to the shiny bone
Of the free original man and woman.

Begin all over again!
From nothing but the pure man
Or woman, as when we were born,
Only this can finally ensure the earth is shorn
Of sophisticated wars of power-broker borderlands;

Let's go back again to the free earth,
Without borders anymore:
Back to that fenceless humanity
And bar-less paradise created by the Lord.

For all things pass
Like a rustle in the grass;
Similarly no borders will last;
The lord ensures that is the case,
In the free laws built into nature,
And into people's innermost consciences;
Freeways nothing can completely erase.

In my travels through life's delightful freeways,
I'll heed "my captain" and break through walls
Erected for us by old cold worldly soulless rulers.
For the pride of a poet won't abide hard borders.

The Old Priest Reflects on a War in the Ukraine

Ballyduff bathes in bright sunshine to welcome St Pat's day,
Bands of nodding narcissi should take winter gloom away,
But Ukraine's war plunges my soul back to winter's despair.

I ask my old priest's view. What's new about war in Europe,
He says, our age endured super-state conflicts before you,
Two senseless wars and untold related smaller sideshows.

Putin's just another monster we conceived in an obscene
Love affair with big states' power and their war machines,
That produces crying offspring of Misses Glory and Greed.

Already in this century Syrian and Iraqi blood's been spilt,
Justified by the old clever propaganda that we've invented,
Implemented by cruel arms, even a nuclear *enlightenment.*

We Irish missed *enlightened* communists and others who,
Preaching secular utopia built paranoid states, sent hoards
Of people to gulag hells at home and on far foreign shores.

Seeing Babels full of human bones in endless *killing fields,*
Shouldn't we seek real change, an alternative era of peace?
Beyond super-state folly and all-justifying secular ideology.

For those who used biological and nuclear arms in our era
Were Putin's kind, western imperialists in two *Great Wars.*
Great? Humanity slaughtered in gas foxholes or Hiroshima.

With Putin we're on the old horror merry-go-round again,
Only postmodern deconstruction can stop this cold killing,
And end super-state war machinery. We can do it if willing.

The alternative is refugee millions fleeing new war crimes.
We can't believe 21st century *progress* is old evils reprised,
But old war technology was kept, powered up, not retired?

So it's inevitable that it's used now by men *who most of all*
Desire power as Tolkien wrote. Stop it! Heed higher calls!
Peace on earth *if we want it* Lennon said, the key's our will.

For if humankind wanted peace it'd have come long since,
A will to do it pursued relentlessly is the only way to peace,
Peace on earth, good will to men, angels spoke perfect sense.

But men will power, even the newest EU super-state seeks
Armies now. Past conflicts should convince us to be meek!
Less rather than more arms heeding God's *Prince of Peace,*

Lest the 21st century be written by Putin in books of death
And our future offspring fail to experience peace on earth,
Let willed lived peace be our aim on the re-greened earth.

If we dream hard and invoke higher aid it can be achieved,
Men changed within, living a peace for which the lord died.
Ending state war machines like that which Christ crucified.

Let his peace in hearts be a path to peace for all who live;
Like Christian convents founded to build *Shalom* inside,
Shalom is a man at peace with himself, nature and his God.

With secular super-state power wars we're lost and blind,
But inner peace in God saves, *enlightens,* makes men wise.
With peace in each heart *hey presto* a peaceful humankind.

Insert Image 6 here

In Praise of Good Books

Early on I loved and avidly devoured every single book
I could lay my hands on; later I learned to discriminate
Books of light from those of darkness, I read to a plan,
Taught by the discriminatory wisdom of the old man.

The finest written word is truly a light-filled highway
To go, it's the soul on the wing the old man taught me:
(*He was my mentor and confidant since I was a baby*):
Good books are a breath of every bludgeoning spring;
Though bad ones may occasionally recall winter chills,
True books teem with bright human life and good will;
They're at the core of humankind's imagining and art;
Individuals come and go; in times of plenty or draught,
Books work to immortalise their finest inner thought;

Books set us apart from passing animal caprice:
The best embody the purest wisdom of the race,
A glory that nothing but the total destruction
Of the earth can deface; and more than that,
When written by divinely inspired prophets,
From a deity within nature's depths and man,
Books are highways to God's timeless immortal land;
From the Karma Sutra to the glories of the Upanishads,
They're lights amid life's night as in the greatest, the Bible:
Followed faithfully it leads us to the open door of paradise;
And on earth it makes us complete inside fair and wise.

But like human beings, there are also bad books:
Books that degrade rather than books that exalt;
Like Mein Kampt that spawned the holocaust,
Books of darkness rather than books of light;
All the yellow and green and dark tomes of terror;

Godless books that led man away from the seven ages
Of humanity's accumulated inner wisdom; stony-hearted
Books that leavened hell in life within even good men,
(*I wish I could get hold of some good comic books,*
I laughed, they'd be a relief from your fanatical talks):

He smiled, and resumed his discourse, unfazed:
Not so are books by ordinary and inspired sages,
Whose pages are dictated by hidden divine muses;
Such books are cathedrals built on rocks of truth;
Such books restore civilizations to their fair youth,
They renew cultures that grow corrupt or uncouth:

Such books continue to open life's glittering door
To the world's great explorers of the mind and soul;
Revealing the depthless possibilities all time holds;
Great books never fade but, with us, they grow old;
They are humankind's diamond dreams set in gold.

If books fade, he continued, for electronic streaming,
Will men and women cease their wondrous dreaming?
Not know themselves or what's really true and good?
Will words serve but passing goals, or only entertain?
Will they shape but amused minds and barren brains?
Oh for books again that leave the soul sighing for more!

Yes, let great books be again! I said; (more than aroused,
I passionately responded to his rich idealistic discourse):
Let good books be, and may the Good Book, *I cried out,*
The book that lights up human life and its glory goals,
Still bring us happiness here and fit us for forever more.

Celebrating the Last Irish Romantic's Isle

Beyond the worm's and an old slave's empire is
Our isle of the storm where lives creativity alive;
Where once lived the soul-wealthy and the wise
Under natural, peaceful and perfect poetic skies;

There this unashamed romantic sings old-style songs,
That filled our days with praise of the free Irishman;
And the presence of a creator lord in his wonder isle:
That like a child's shining eyes can never be destroyed.

I live there still and see "his blood upon the rose";
In this green isle of dreams where every day we've
A sky audience for symphonies of peace, and wires
And groves are violins played by wild rainy winds;

There drums are white waves battering the rocks;
Plucked guitars are the patter of endless raindrops;
There French horns are the honking of rock seals;
And in green fields ring bells of holy spring wells;

There seagull cries are tolling from church towers;
And it is as every man is deep in his seeking soul;
Where even rain and sleet and cold are our friends;
Visionary hearts see old glittering gold in all things;

Our shores are by seas of beauty glorious to behold;
Our roads run to high coastal cliffs of forever more:
Our wings of birds soar over rarest Burren flowers;
Our majestic mountains are high as heaven's towers;

Ah yes, the Ireland of the poets is a bird of eternal days,
The old man said; (his deeply-felt words I had to praise,
They kept resonating in my mind for many future days);
Yes I replied, praised forever by poetry, our island's mother!

II

But aren't you praising an idealised nature and Ireland
Is it long past? I said, isn't that glory and beauty now lost
To the cold light of reality, downgraded on every hand?
Haven't we abandoned nationalist ancestors' dream land?

Sadly yes, the old man said, yet let me argue with Wilde,
That art shouldn't be a mirror of reality, but reality of art;
The isle our ancestors dreamed in free hearts is more
Real than an alien imported one now imposed by Dublin 4.

The cynics and iconoclasts, like dogs, will have their day,
But may the island our ancestors dreamed not pass away.
Anyway, as Saussure shows, life is a construct, so let it be
A construct of art, not an edifice of cold reductive history;

As the old man said this I praised the wisdom that in old age
He'd acquired; I said aesthetes are right, let art be a fine tool
To assail and defeat a spreading night of destroyed dreams;

And may they let the church be, the core of rare Irish being".
But wasn't the church, I said, often cruel in autocratic rule
And abuse? Yes, but its deep mystery kept Christ's humility,
A godly integrity that gave us spiritual and family stability;
Crimes and suicides were few in our young community;
An imperfect church is still soul health for Paddy's own;
Lest souls, empty here, wander lost on vast eternal shores.

The Task of the Aesthete

The old man continued
His train of aesthetic musing:
If the glory of art is beauty,
What is the glory of beauty?
God, source of great natural creations,
And what's grand and enduring in nations.
So what then is the poet's vocation?
It was a question I could answer:
Beauty, I cried, to bring it forth
In pain and labour, like a bonny baby;
To recreate the earth in a faithful art, that
Incarnates man's godly imaginative heart!

To create colours and forms
So intensely lovely, they live on,
And so intensely truthful
They embody reflections
Of Christ who is God's good son,
The eternal Word, from whose hand sprung
Untold wonders, when the earth was young.

Poets as masters of the word
Have an on-going share in that, by creating
Word glory that reflects humanity's greatness
And the grandeur with which nature gifts us.

But when you dedicate your
Life to such art, what do you do
If it all seems to fail and fall apart?
His questions were getting harder:
What if your art's not good enough?

You dig deeper into your heart and soul,
I replied coldly, irked by what he implied:
You work to bring out those pure perfect forms
They were placed within us by the Creator lord.

The Poet Explores a Starry Universe Within (the last frontier?)

There is a universe in you and me:
An inner universe, the old man said.
A cosmos scattered with galaxy on galaxy,
Of glorious inspired divinity;
Moments of emotional intensity;
Planet on planet of irrepressible plans,
And black holes of imaginative immensity.

There is a universe in you and me:
Myriads of moons of mystery,
And billions of starry thoughts,
Struggling to be and to be free.

There is a universe in you and me:
Meteorite showers of powerful desires,
And comets trailing into inspirations
That would reach the outer rim of infinity;

There is a universe in you and me:
Faraway space worlds of dreams,
Shining pearly planes of compressed energy,
And streaming falling meteors of diamond invention;
Bright Venuses and morning stars of dazzling hopes,
And the heart's northern star guiding us home to truth.

There is a universe in you and me:
Love passions as of Venus and Jove;
And Saturns of musical strings and songs;
And milky ways of wedding rings,
Where every woman and every man,
Swims in the skies of love's divine plan.

There is a universe in you and me:
A universe of art and beauty set free,
Of black holes of depthless science;
And the miracles of medicinal advances;
And like the endless space of the universe above us,
There's a sea of starry feeling in the heart within us.

But as Einstein said, I replied
We can live our lives as if nothing is a miracle,
Or as if everything is a miracle;
The world is a miracle,
That's the heart of the mystery;
We can keep our eyes closed to life's glory,
Or we can open them to far skies and seas
Of immense spatial milky ways of creativity.
For there is a vast universe in you and me,
And in poetry's cosmic vision unto eternity.

The Maze to Life

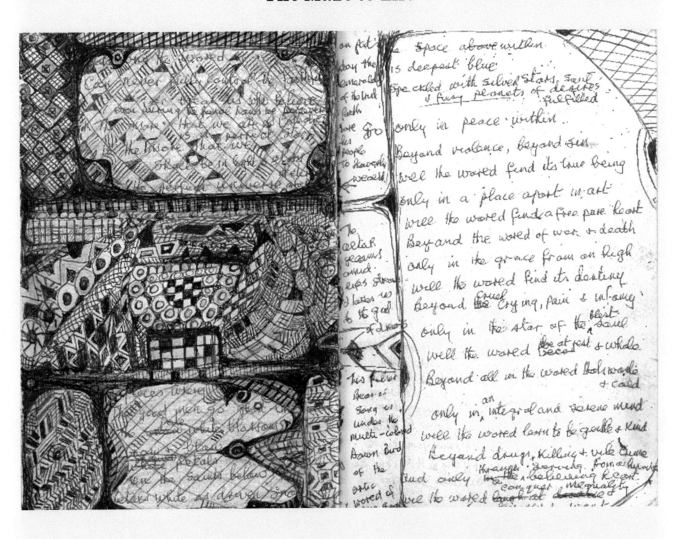

The Awakening

"I wake from sleep and take my waking slow" - Roethke

The night's bright as a gemstone;
Its cry as faint a child's moan
At the moment of birth;
The night is still as a bone;
Its skeleton is as lifeless
As the reconstructed hypothesis
Of Neanderthal man;
The night is calm as a cradle;
Its child is as soundless
As a mother tip-toeing in
To see that all is all right;

But eventually the night wakes up:
Its cock crows; its dawn screams.
As night's blood is shed by the sun,
I must rise reluctantly,
And suffer for that crime;
For the dawn darkens the night,
Killing its soul, its diamond dreams,
With the bloody onset of enlightenment;

Like Callista surprising Diana,
And she gathering her robes
Around her to shield her nakedness,
(See Titian's painting of the same),
The dawn shocks the night awake:
Blazing like a forest fire;
Raging up out of the darkness
Without warning it cajoles us
Into facing the glare of a new garish reality;

The dawn is a cock crowing;
The dawn sparkles the floor
Of night like a multi-faceted jewel;
Brilliant ruby-red, bloody and cruel;

Lady dawn steps out of her night dress
Clad only in the pearly pyjamas of day;
The dawn in-rocks the serenity of night
With sharp loud rhythms of pop drums;

Its long-haired singer erupts
Out of the darkened stage:
Carrying the microphone of morning,
He screams his thunderous rock song
Into the ear-phones of a reeling universe;

The dawn darkens the pure peaceful night,
Of quiet and sleep and sweetest dreaming;
Making me face the colder realities of being:
Out of a soft blessed blanket-street blindness,
My eyes pop wide open; it's a woke awakening!

Man or Machine

Are you a man or a machine?
The old man, my muse, said to me;
He had this yen against computers
And word-processors and such like.

I think I'm still human, I replied,
Though I'm constantly
On the mobile phone,
And on the computer day and night;

I sometimes think it invents
Conundrums to keep me on it for hours on end
For days even. I think I am still human,
Though I'm not as sure of that as I used to be;
Sometimes a twitch comes into my hand
At the vibrating and flashing of a computer screen,
And I seem to hear Alexa's mechanical voice
Reciting obscure facts and numbers in my dreams;

A computer trying to answer
My deepest questions, it's stupid!
I think I have stopped being human
Some time ago, the old man said;
Maybe that's why I feel dead
And gone to the great Computer
Scrap heap in the sky;

He laughed, and so did I.
Yet for the rest of the day
He haunted me;
His question was now my question,
Am I a man or a machine?

Suddenly, I seem to hear a creaking in my bones
And I'm tempted to get an oil can
To make me walk smoothly again;
And I sometimes think I need anti-rust
To stop my increasingly metal mind seizing up;

Throw it away! The old man said,
With a grin, as I sat before the computer
For most of the day; throw it away!
Or it will take you over like sin;
And then you'll be unable
To become human ever again.

Yes, I replied, and if I became a machine,
What'd happen to the Ghost in the machine?
Would it be deleted, dumped in the trash bin?

The World and Banksy

He sat in the café sighing,
The old man with the silver hair;
Beside him a child was crying
For a dog run over by a car;

Blood was everywhere,
Under a Banksy mural
Of two boys looking furtively
At a naked lady in a shower;

I saw there both life's cruelty
And art's transcendent sanity.

Return to Dreaming

"My paintings come to me as in a dream" – Van Gogh

When the world's cold winds
Batter my window,
Dreams flesh my brain,
White with the fear
That their grace might fail,
And leave me in a night of the soul.

No! At the brink
Of that jagged cliff,
Let my glistening eyes,
Contemplate the great leap
Into the hallowed core
Of the depthless dreaming soul.

There some diamond dream,
In a secret womb, is waiting to unfold,
A baby beyond the world's dying night;
A child growing in the heart,
Crying for birth into living art.

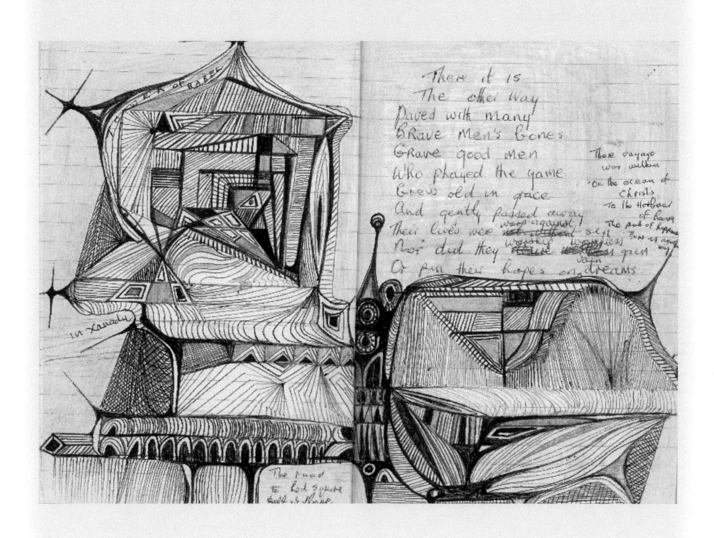

There it is
The other way
Paved with many
Brave men's bones
Grave good men
Who played the game
Grew old in grace
And gently passed away
Their lives were [illegible] against [illegible]
Nor did they worship [illegible]
Or pin their hopes on dreams

The Light of Poetry and Art

When the darkest night descends,
And pain is in my every sense,
Books of poetry and works of art,
Manage to make the dark depart.

They satisfy the heart and like music
Of the spheres harmonize the mind;
In times of tears they gently console;
In life's emptiness they nourish me inside;

For poetic art reverses humanity's fall:
Its heaven's gift sent to some, for all;
It's a good wife, a cask of gold to hoard;
It echoes the eternal creativity of the Lord;

Its word-joys conspire to make my humanity whole,
And open gates to light-filled fields of forever more.

The Maturing Poet's Sees Art's Dilemmas

To be an artist
Is to suffer again and again:
At not being recognised,
At being over-recognised,
At being vulgarised,
At being misunderstood,
At being too analysed and so not enjoyed,
At being plagiarised,
At never reaching the great prize,
The supreme work
That will really open people's eyes.

To be an artist of the soul
Is an even more challenging enterprise;
For it is to be a disciple of Christ,
Or some other supreme seer of the soul;
It's to seek to be good and true and whole;
For the variety, colour and complexity
Of the world proves that God is an artist of infinite depth,
And to attempt to reflect that is a poet's duty from birth.

To be an artist is to be open to the endless surprise
Of God's greatest work of art, that is humankind:
An artist should glory in the wealth in the human mind;
And a heavenly spirit shining from men and women's eyes;
Even as this poet is old in vain fallen flesh and failing eyes,
He still aspires, in occasional inspired times, fewer now,
To create sunny skies of truth, soaring over the clay webs
Of the world, the flesh and an evil one's entangling lies.

To be an artist of the soul is to be a voice
Crying in a wilderness of one's own searching soul;
That voice says: "Come back to God and be whole".

It is a voyage alone to a universe so fine
It cannot but last for it heals the world's sighs;
It shows it the peaceful and immortal ways
Of the creative Trinity; may it ever be praised!

In my life loving friends and family most reflect the Trinity.

The Old Man's Similes of Humility

Like dog-roses on an Irish hedge;
Let me endure the turned up noses
Of the haughtier garden breed;

Like a feed of fish and chips,
Or a bag of falafel,
Let me sit in the market place
Among donkeys and flies
As my arrogant ego dies;

Like a salad of sweet herbs,
Let me eat St Peter's fish
In Galilee and admire the fires
Of evening under silvery stars;

Like white sandal socks
On the feet of schoolgirls,
Let me ever renew youthfulness;

Like Johnny Walker
On the rocks of New York
Let me taste the honey whiskey of Cork.

Like a pencil-parer in a dull desk
Let me sharpen my slack senses,
With ever more vibrant poetic inventions.

Like a wastepaper basket in a busy office
Let me gather the papers of prosperity
Which are my best poems for posterity;

Like an eraser on the sketch pad of a maturing artist
Let me learn wasteful tastefulness, vanity rubbed away,
May I leave to posterity pale gains of my frail dying clay.

The Squirrel

I saw the squirrel
Of my lonely heart,
Rooting in the forest of art,
For the sacred acorns
Of beauty and truth.

And what he unearthed
Was the great cross
Of the lord Jesus Christ,
Embossed with rubies of his blood
And emeralds of his word,
And the twisted gold and silver
Of his eternal youth and fervour.

And my heart burst
With all that I could encompass
Of his wisdom, joy and light.
And round about the forest of my heart,
Snow white anemones of spring
Bloomed more and more,
Like the embroidered robe
Of Mother Mary,
As she welcomed me at heaven's door.

And I cast at her feet
My illuminated notebooks
Of many a lonely night;
And she turned them into eternal life;
And she said you are wise,
For the only things that satisfy
The heart for good,
Are love, art and God.

And I saw the acorn of God grace
Within my soul,
Growing into a towering oak in Christ,
Until it would reach the blue heavens
And inaccessible light.

There is a simple Trinity in me
Mind & Soul
& Body
There is a Trinity in me
Hand and pen & poetry

_____

There they are overleaf.
My special Trinity
Not patriarchal
But, femininity
Not a bearded man
with a stern face
But smiling young women
with the joy of grace
When God ushers me
into eternity
This will be my everlasting mission
My joyful
Beatific vision

THE TRINITY

More Poems of a Personal Spiritual Odyssey

When in youth, as I grew apace,
Every good thing the lord did for me
Gave me an inkling of his immensity and grace.

But it is a long time since I was twenty,
And a longer time still since I was twelve,
But the velvet hand I felt then still touches me;
Like when I slipped out of teens
Into an Institute given to the God of my dreams.

That faded for a while, but it's curious that at forty
I should again fall under that spell,
And at fifty-six draw water from a well
I had drawn sparsely from in my mid-years.

For the hard institutionalism of Maynooth
Nearly knocked that devotedness out of me,
But now as I'm an old priest, instead of growing cold,
My heart has begun to swell again in that old love,
And I say once more I give all to you O Christ forever more!

Vision

The other day while in prayer,
The old man declared,
In faith I thought I saw
Before me a golden door,
Leading to the heavens of God,
And Christ enthroned in grandeur there.

The vision was more than I could bear,
For to that door a stair led,
But one I dare not mount,
Being not yet wrapped up in death.

"Let me but go", I said,
Up that stairs to the tower
Where you are,
To walk among the blessed dead,
The white-robed saints that worship
You there, free of earthly care and strife".

"Your state of flesh is
Yet to be dissolved", he said;
"Your task on earth
Is a work in progress.
It is as yet but incomplete.
We will meet later", he said,
"Beyond the great silver gate
Where heaven's glories wait".

I felt like debating with him,
Saying let this be my natal date
Into that paradise of sinless bliss;
But bowing to his will instead,
I kissed the hem of his cloak,

And went once more restored
Among men, cherishing that vision
Of that golden door and stair
That awaited me when my time had come,
And the voice of the Lord called me home.

II

The following night I had a vision;
An angel spoke to me
These words of warning:
"We do not realise what demons
Wait in hiding to surprise us?
What protection from the saints
And from the angels of God we have
If we ask! But we must ask
For we are free. Foolish is the man
Who thinks he can defeat
The evil host by his own strength.

It's never too late, halt and take softly
The hand of Love, and be safe, happy
And totally at peace within, Goodbye!"
I realised it was my guardian angel
Who shone on me a great blazing light
As I gazed into the visions of the night.

Human Rights and Free Speech

What is vision
Other than
The vastness of God?
What is wisdom
Other than
Heeding his voice?
What is truth
Other than
Unravelling his mind?
What is his home?
Other than
Glory unconfined?
What is his duty
Other than eternal beauty?
What is his mind
Other than infinite designs?
What are human rights
Other than God's ways?
What is freedom of speech
Other than God's Praise?

Writing is Being

Poetry happens alone
When alone at night
You write,
With nothing between you
And the darkness
But an electric light:

And the stone of time
Is pressing down,
And the meaninglessness
Of the bare bone,
And you hurt inwardly
And cannot be healed;

Then you are alone
With your divine muse,
And you reach up your hand
And he takes it.
In the bliss of burning words,
You pass over life's deep abyss.
And stumble into paradise;

Alone at night in the ambit
Of a small bedside electric lamp;
I cry: I write therefore I am.

The combinations
the separate aspects
And permutations
of the mind
Are met by the freedom
of the heart
And the depth
And infinity
of the Imagination
And what of the colour
And pleasure
of Sensation,
ALL ordered
Are are found in the
& configured
Breadth & beauty
of Xt the LORD

Remembering in Age the Birds of a Country Boy's Youth

You were the birds
That sang to me,
When I was young,
From our sycamore tree.
And every note
Was true and clear,
And sang each morning into being.

Down the road
Of life I ran,
When the sun
Was rising in the sky.
And every bird
Sang for me,
And I wished that
I could sing as freely.

For my soul was then
Like them,
A being lately sprung from eternity.

Seeing the World Differently

We must see the world differently,
The old man said to me suddenly,
Each creature as an immense mystery,
And an aspect of divinity,
As untold great cultures saw things in the past,
Wearing animal and bird masks.
Alas science cruelly rid us westerners
Of a sense of life's unfathomable inwardness.
It's not an abstract entity to be analysed;
That's all right as a device of progress,
But we must go beyond logic
To insight into spiritual nature of nature and humanity,
Like Coleridge or Hopkins who saw the "inscape" of reality.
We must penetrate beyond the surface
To the eternal edifice, underlying
And supporting all things, the soul of life.
The inner living delight of all things let's realise,
All the glory that lies under the surface of mere sight.
It was my old man's song: each person or natural entity,
Is a piece of fine poetry, an echo of the universal divinity.

The Black bird

Thus I adored an ecological icon, my blackbird of song.
In an era of global warming and lost flora and fauna,
Happily, he knows nothing of human cruelty or wrong.
I saw him as living, breeding and saying *my being is song*:
"*I just am what I was created to be, true to my given role,*
I'm black, wild, and happily free from man's tortured mind;
I just fly in the sky, feed and each spring propagate my kind".

He's a masterpiece from the Lord's studio, a study in black,
A work in progress in an epic poem of the universal book.
Bringing joy to us humans as we wander in the woods,
Or pause, jogging, on a path to enjoy a joyous flood
Of melody; there's rare pure goodness in his airy singing,
His dignified bearing, and his happy affirmation of being.

His brown wife's a wonder in a home of twigs and moss,
She incubates dutifully a clutch of sky-blue spotted eggs;
A batch of black and brown birds she fasts to allow to be,
Doing a motherly duty for earth's future and you and me.
Beyond the cruel greed and war of "reasonable" humanity.

I write
Therefore I am
And so the saints of God
As well as the damned of hell
Envy me
I write and dream of the best
Therefore I am for the rest in silence
And so the soaring angels of song
As well as the chained demons of
                              disharmony
Envy me
I write and foresee free art
                              in Christ
Therefore I am alive,
And so the blossoming young of
                              earth
As well as the dying old of heaven
Envy me   today
I write in sheer delight in song
                              agin
Therefore I ....
And so the saintly scholars of life
As well as the ignorant dead
  Envy me
Who being free, alive & wise ....

The Ostrich

Of all the exotic birds I early on read about in books
To me the ostrich always seemed the clown of birds,
As, like Beckett, his profile sharply pondered
The absurd, or plunged like Winnie in sands
Without guile, persuading himself, like her
That all our days were happy, that not looking
At troubles will make them go away post haste.
Hiding his precious talents in sandy seas,
In shallow nests where predators feast, he seems
Doomed to perpetual blundering, all at sea
Among the ships of the desert and white-robed sheiks
Sipping mint tea. In the rational reality of us boys
And our cruelty, he seemed too innocent and unwise.
Yet round and smooth as a pearl and big as a rock,
This unwise ostrich's egg seems to lock
Within it the silver and gold of the world.
Out of it creeps the clumsy bird's brood
Into baking sun, rudely awake to mother's folly
And falling into the same trap of being born
In a wilderness of sand, of having been shorn
Of the green shade and woods of saner birds,
Where among foliage and forests of sustaining
Slugs and seeds, they warbled a simpler life away.
Without a song, yet still under the care of God
Even in desert desolation, the ponderous ostrich
Somehow survives and breeds and grows taller
And swifter afoot than all the other birds;
Shaping itself in the form and the original fashion
Of the universal egg, and magical in its stately action.
To amaze and please us God gives all nature and nations Dear images of deity,
creations of soul-satisfying beauty.

I Envy the Slimness of the Wagtail

Even more fascinating is the dapper dashing wagtail,
His vocation to entertain, he carries out without fail.

Ever dancing this way or that, his sin is to stay still.
Indeed, his pecking and his tail wags are all so fast,
We ask is he a bird at all, or a blue-and-white ghost?

Who not needing to nest, was born of and lived off dust.
Which'd explain how his slimness survives winter rain,
Snow, and frost 'til plentiful summer came around again,

Unlike Buddha, he is far too busy to ever enjoy being fat.

The King of All Birds

As wise and engaging is the tiny wren king,
Difficult to see in the recesses of furze
Bushes, and more difficult still to catch,
On high scratchy thrones in thorn trees,
Where his haughty highness, sits displeased,
Condemning the treason of wild wanton boys.

For every St. Stephen's day we pretended
We'd captured him, dressed in as absurd
A rag-tag stage costume as we could find,
And chanting at each Boher house, to gain
Some pennies to cast off winter's dark reign:

"The wran, the wran, the king of all birds,
St. Stephen's day he was caught in the furze,
Up with the kettle and down with the pan,
A penny or two to bury the wran". If we knew
The woman of the house we'd add in unison:
"Mrs Murphy's a very good woman, a very good
Woman, she'll give us a penny to bury the wran"

A ritual to restore the lost sun to us was just fun.
Why anyone wanted to bury the tiny green bird,
Committing birdicide to do so, to us was absurd,
Our young consciences rebelled. We just feigned
Regicide to get money to celebrate Christ's birth.

The Penguin of the Soul

The penguin of the soul
Learns to live in the great worldly cold,
And thrive and feed and breed.

The penguin of the soul
Clusters with others to stay warm;
He knows he can't do it on his own.

The penguin of the soul
Waits patiently for all icy storms to pass,
Bending and letting blizzards go over his communal back.

The penguin of the soul
Keeps his young safe from icy blasts, and fasts
Until his partner takes over the future-nurturing task.

The penguin of the soul
Does not hoard or worry or go to war,
He just follows a snow order ordained for him by the lord.

The wren is singing for me
Wearing his crown of light
Amid the thorny trees of life
He brings me a melody of bright
Simplicity, why then should I cry.
His tiny green body is a piping fife
To sing away all my sorrows these
Be at peace, he says to my soul
To live & sing is enough
To be just ourselves is the stuff
Dreams are made of, look up
Sing on and do not be afraid
To thank God for this gift
of life's green singing bird.
Life may be absurd in many ways
But being a thing of beauty
          and song is not.
Lets just celebrate that with wit
and with gratitude in our heart

Lost Time

Every morning as I rise,
And gaze in the mirror,
I see Satan gazing at me
With bloodshot eyes.

And every night I lie down to sleep
Is like lying in my grave;
I am afraid.
All the things I didn't do that day
Or I haven't done in life
Seem to rant and rave
To keep me awake.

For every night's sleep
Is another nail
In my coffin.
And all the while
The devil is laughing.

Escape to the Wild

"Come away O human child
To the waters and the wild,
With a fairy hand in hand,
For the world's more full of weeping
Than you can understand" – W B Yeats

I've often dreamed, the old man said,
Of leaving that world, going apart; like Yeats,
Or like the first hermits fleeing into the desert;
Maybe I was born in the wrong age.

I have dreamed of living in wild places:
With a few acres; building a shelter
With my own hands, growing enough
To keep me going; and with someone,

A woman, who would share my bare lot:
Keeping a few cows, or a goat;
And growing vegetables and hens
For eggs; and a little plot of wheat

To beat into flour and make bread;
Then I would no longer live off plastic and tech;
I'd return to my country roots and regain a peace I lack.

The Banksy of Christianity

I am the Banksy of the Lord.
On every wall I would paint his word
Away with darkness, away with the sword.

I am the Banksy of his humane Christ.
As I watch a dying sun in the west, on renewed forests
I'd carve his call to come home to God and find soul rest.

I am the Banksy of Mother Mary.
By high tramway graffiti routes I'd write the *Memorare;*
On backstreet gables the peace-love message of Our Lady.

I am the Banksy of the Holy Ghost.
On church entrances I would paint a mural of the lost
Returning, led by the dove, to a church of the eternally just.

I am the Banksy of all the saints trice blessed.
On slum walls I'd paint their work for justice on earth,
The white-robed throng marching in to an eternal rebirth.

I am the Banksy of the angels of God in bright array.
I'd paint their wings of light on every ad-board display,
Their harps of joy on every plane flying across the sky.

I am the Banksy of the legions of lay devout.
I would paint them in relief on walls by every bus route,
Enjoying the rewards of a well-earned heavenly banquet.

II

Alas if I am lost on death's dark sea
With poems on the shore still waiting for me!
Alas if I'm tossed into the sea of eternity
With poems in time still pleading with me!
"Come and let us be in time pearls of earthly poetry,
Let us be, among your doodles of destiny,
The bright Banksys of painted Christianity".

Alas let me not be lost in death's dark sea
With doodles and poems below calling to me!
Crying infants of art aching and panting to be.

Wise Kindness

"Thou should'st not have been old 'til thou had'st been wise" – King Lear

The best gifts are from the heart
The old man said, his eyes alive
Though his body was dead:
I took his hand, he was my grandfather
And had given me everything all my life;
A love and kindness of heart towards others
That is not just Christian but a universal value
Of faith and life (the old man said believe me son,
Faith without loving charity is dust and ashes at last);
The Dali Lama sums up all faith as "warm-heartedness":

We overstress money now, the old man continued,
But our true riches are in our humaneness;
Kindness is the God within
And cancels all our sins;
Love *is* the human being;
It's the only thing that matters in the end:
Even the secular pop world recognizes this;
"All you need is love", the Beatles' song refrain,
At his words, echoed like a mantra in my brain.
The ad media create "wants", with clever convincing lies,
But we can live without such things but not without love,
Without that the heart, even faith, shrivels up and dies.

The following day the old man died:
He had been unable to speak for two years;
As I looked into his dead eyes, I knew
My entry to eternal happiness was his legacy,
It was in the wealth of warm love he'd left me.

The Spirit of Place

Each place has a soul,
The old man said:
Some of the spirit
Of the people who lived
When you and I were young
Still linger in the fields,
And walk the roads,
And climb the mountains wild,
And toil behind the plough,
And sow and reap the crops,
And still go to mass in horses and traps.

Places have souls, like my own Lamanaugh:
Generations of Buckleys
Have left their mark on the land;
Their footsteps still thread the soil,
Their souls still dance on feet
On the old boards of the family house,
Now a ruin, the abode of rats and mice.
But voices sound in the weed-grown rooms
And hands still hold and whisper of love
In the beds of moss and grass:
"We lived here and made it our heart.
It is still a part of us though we rot in clay
Under a grey granite stone,
Occasionally our spirits return
To haunt our old home:
And play cards on the table that's no longer there;
And sit before the turf fire;
And hunt the rabbit and the fox and the hare;
And feed and milk the cows,
And help them calve in the stall behind the house;

And clean out the manure and put it in heaps
To be put out in autumn as well-rotted compost,
To naturally fertilise the land".

I hear the spirits of 8 children, 8 boys
Playing in the haggard among ridges
Of carrots, parsnips, potatoes and cabbage,
Harvested in the summer and eaten
With carefully cured bacon for organic feasts.

In the fireplace among buachalans
The woman of the house still heaps coals
On a black oven for baking bread,
Hung on a crane over the open fire,
As her husband picks a red coal to light his pipe,
And sits in the lamplight reading
The poems of his cousin Ned Buckley,
From a thin red book sold at Knocknagree fair.

The accordion music of Denis Connors
Still sounds here at Stations, surrounded by neighbours.
Ghost jigs and reels like the roots of trees going deep.
Time has moved on but as long as their offspring
The Buckley clan carry on remembering,
The place's grace will live on and sing forever more,
Like the birds that sang for us on our tall sycamores.

II

Once when my world was dark with desire
And full of pain and loss,
I sat again before that old turf fire
Beside Lamanaugh cross,
And said the dead are with me here
And all the love I miss.
And I said in this place my soul's at peace,
Though the rest of the world is lost
In death, the violent taking of human life,
As it seeds war's devastation on the earth.

Free from all that, lay me down at last in Cullen,
Where birds still sing sweetly in the rowan trees,
Plover feed peacefully forever in the clover fields,
And a nearby Araglen washes away my life's tears.

Discovery of Love in Palestine

(from a series of love poems written in Palestine where I lectured in Bethlehem U)

It's Christmas Eve and Jean
In red, is like a radiant
Child of Eve;
What can aid me if she smile?
Or as Santa Clause give presents
And embraces, at mass
In the Nativity nave;

The winter stars are bright as
The star over the manger,
Strangely it snowed heavily
This Christmas Eve;
Jean is snow white too,
A prayer of beauty above
All vain elements of clay,
Red as blood or flame,
Pink as femininity;

As stars are bright
Here, so is Jean, in
The cold night warmed with hymns
In the sacred Nativity Square,
And in the cave nearby
Where she and I go to pray
Before images of Mary and Joseph
Holding their baby boy;

I know that I, a poor professor
Of a higher celibate love,
Shouldn't be too close to her,
Thinking of purposes beyond prayer,

But the moonlit winter night is a temptress
And so is Jean,
In a furry cap and coat and gloves
Of Christmas red,
Kneeling there,
Before the lord
Of the living and the dead;

She kisses that body
Image of the infant, placed
In the manger on a red cloth
Beneath gold and silver
Orthodox icons,
With incense filling the air,
Silently, I imagine her saying,
This is love's holy little boy, he
Is free and fair as the starry sky
That shines over the sacred city
Of Bethlehem this special night.

Snow Peace in Palestine

Love Scene

The scene we inhabit
Jean, is a painted
Japanese silk screen:
You and I near the top,
The backdrop below
Of tiered ink wood,
Ochre leaves, and blue
Stylised streams.

We wander along these
Parchment mountainy passes,
Hand in hand; a faint breeze
Ruffles your ink-dark hair;
The air is high and clear,
Beside a twisted tree, a fountain
Throws up crystal drops
Of glass into our eyes;
In the distance,
The sun is blood red,
In gold/vermilion skies.

Remember it all;
Paint its passion, I said,
In old rolled vellum,
Before it fades,
And all are empty lazy days.

Lost Dreams

Jean in the green wood
Seems to dream her life away.
I see rain falling about her
In grey Glasgow
As she seeks a new way;
And I think of sun-drenched Palestine
And the many days we talked
In the flat below Beit Jala.

And the black cat you fed
Out of kindness, that kept
Coming and going to be stroked,
While we were growing together
And fading apart.

Past the Suk at midnight
I still see your red coat
Floating on Christmas Eve;
Your face weaving
Patterns of smiles
On the winter face of Bethlehem.

God took my heart,
And the Intifada
Took you to England,
And then to Glasgow.

When will our wandering cease?
When will we both be at peace?
When will I cease to wish and weep,
Nights as I toss in restless sleep?

Easter in Jerusalem

Easter liturgies in Jerusalem were feasts for the soul, enjoyed in all of our senses;
No bible-alone church puritan Reformation Platonist Sparseness and emptiness:
But various colourful chants and everywhere smoky clouds of scented incenses,
Leaving us as drugged worshippers reeling in colourfully-tiled ornate chapel aisles,
Beguiled and mesmerised by magnificent multi-sect sights melodies and bell chimes.
Unlike western cynics we weren't scandalised by the Resurrection Church's bedlam,
Our eyes and minds gloried in being dazzled by processions of gold and silver icons,
And by the riot of embroidery and glamour in splendid and grand gilded vestments;
And gold candles of every shape and size in the hands of rich-robed chanting priests.

Later we retreated to a related riot of pilgrims and their priests in the Via Dolorosa:
Hymns in cacophonous tongues attacking our ears as we shouldered Christ's cross,
By the scents of side traders selling spices and boys haranguing us to buy rosary beads;
Up steep stairs of an all-selling Suk we toiled with other hymn-singing pilgrims,
To a Roman Orthodox mass and the sweet taste of the communion and blessed bread,
As we revelled in droning millennium-old Greek Liturgies from cradles of Christianity;
The glorious insanity of conflicting Copt, Armenian and Syrian Orthodox harmonies
Ring from jealously-guarded arbours of various eternally adorned Basilicas of worship,
Rushes of soulful fervour contrary to the pale indifference of western snap-shot tourists.
There I realised the road to God has no vicarious bounds set by nation, colour or logic,
For man is a sensuous animal and the glorious variety of his creation also exists
In the vital religious field, as in Jerusalem's fleshly sights and sounds and aromas,
Praising a Word made Flesh called by narrower souls a glutton and a wine-drinker.

Hosts of bells ring, and candles small and tall, thin and fat, white and coloured,
Smelling of a fiery belief, glow gold in aisles of the icon-rich Church of the Angels.
There we sing St James's ancient liturgy, a feast for our eyes, ears and noses,
And drink sweet scented wine transposed by the priest into the blood of Christ.
We go home joyful, blessed by Jerusalem's incarnation of soul, its Easter sense feast.

Snowstory Feb. 1992.
— To Bethlehem

The snow is falling
Around my mind
Blind cold flakes falling
In a silent
Windless night on Bethlehem
I sit in the light
And with it piling
By the wall of thought
The enwrought iron gate
Of ignorance is already white
So is the fence of disbelief
It heaps up against the brawn
Bark of death
Heavy with clay breathing
Against the wet pane
It beats & slides to rest
Already the road to Beit Jola
Is marked with tracks of motor feet
To the heights of Judah
And Jerusalem the storm sweeps on
With whispers of peace
Here along at dawn
I pray this snow may
        never cease

The Black and the Grey Cat

Two wild cats come to my door:
The grey cat is calm
And sits like a Buddha,
Incapable of being alarmed;
I call him Gandalf the Grey,
For it suits his wise appearance.
By contrast the black cat
Is furiously active and acquisitive.
From the two I realised
Animals too have unique personalities.

When I throw out some food
A comic interplay soon ensues:
I throw in one place,
The black cat pushes
The grey out of the way and eats
Both shares ravenously;
I throw elsewhere,
The black cat leaves his food
And rushes to again push the grey away.
The grey turns to the food Blackie's left,
But the black immediately rushes to push him aside.
Though occasionally the grey trusts out
A disapproving claw, he lets it be,
For essentially he is a cat of peace
And sociable sharing and tranquillity.

I throw food all over,
And the black is reluctantly
Forced to share,
For he can't be everywhere at the same time.
But I can see that he's annoyed

At the thwarting plan I've devised;
Hence he eats as fast as he can
So that he can rush again,
To deprive the grey of at least
Some of the prize,
He's gained by my ruse.

Surely men are also like that:
All are shades variously
Of either the black or the grey cat.

Life is Sweet When We Show it White Teeth

The antidote to life's suffering is laughter,
It is God's most beautiful daughter,
The old man said with a titter,
The grin is the queen of everyone;
When we can laugh at ourselves
We can live with ourselves,
And waltz into heaven on the wings of a smile;
Life is sweet when we show it white teeth.

Yes, I have always thought
That God loves a clown,
And laughs at man's folly,
And gives him a soul at its best when jolly;
Life is sweet when we show it white teeth.

How is it that when young we cry easily,
But later we hardly cry at all,
Or ever laugh, until we can cry;
Life is sweet when we show it white teeth.

Is the role of the poet then
To escape from stern joyless men
Who, for control, would contain our gladness
And prevent us from living
In the warmth of God's laughter;
Laugh at them and they'll have no power over us anymore;
For as in Shakespeare the clown is an anarchist,
And there deflates even a king's grave self-importance;
Life is sweet when we show it white teeth.

Life is full of love in Christ;
Life is white wings
And snowy doves of trust,

Of truth, of stainless absurd sinless smiling
Youth, alive under the sun that is God's free laughter;
Life is sweet when we show it white teeth.

Ah, our infinite belief is never too late!
That life can still be clean and crystal as a child's dream,
And happy as the prattle of a child's laughter;
Or as full of expectant wishes as the rattle of dinner dishes.
Life is sweet when we show it white teeth.

The Old Man's Word Play on Time's Tyranny

Time moves on and leaves us deep in the ground;
We're ground into dust by time and violent times.
We can't dust ourselves off, in grave defiance say,
"I'm OK"; such defiance is just useless nonsense.
It makes no sense, time still winks and marches on;
And chill March winds will not stop to sigh over us,
Nor will golden trees unleave to cover us in glory;

We cannot even glory in what gold we leave behind;
Behind our backs someone will squander it and smile.
Youth finds a way to treat us as comical past matters.
No matter if we'd defy time our time or times will pass:

Past memories, past hair, past fire, a last age of loneliness.
Even loneliness of the long distance runner won't remain;
Our remains just decay to bone under a cold grey stone;
And stone hearts pass by without a prayer, sigh or thought,
Who has ever thought that time ever condescends to care.
In life it didn't care less if we survived or if we meekly died.
When the die is cast at last our puny moment rushes by,
Time and frail times just rush meekly to memory's night,
And no three sisters knit the night anew. Church chimes,
The chimes of time, peal to celebrate busy worms of time,

Wait old man I said, maybe you've been far too hard on time.
Surely poets and artists pile scorn on time by ageless art,
Or in the art of procreation children carry on our seed,
They in turn seeding our name are tiny victories over time.

Yes, he said, as charted in the Times or TV crime shows,
Time also seeds man's crimes, evil fills time's course.
Of course what most occurs in time are wars for power,
Lust for land or wealth informs history's conflicts forever.

This is too negative I said, there's also progress beyond time,
The progress we gain from the heritage of past great minds.
Each age gains from past art and science, life now
Builds on past fruitful gains, it is more than a frail game,
There's also goodness, grace and beauty amid pain and loss,
And to offset time's passage, let's use the time given to us.

Alone at Night

Alone at night listening to clocks
On a bed as leaden minutes move by,
I remain calm, I cry out, I am alive;
I write, therefore I am.

Because only in me
Everything is, when I die
Everything will be gone, I foolishly surmise.
I alone see, hear, touch, taste, smell,
I alone think and in a dream mostly float
In time's stream aimlessly, except when I write?
I write therefore I am.

Am even I real, really here?
Yet alone at night sitting on a bed
Listening to clocks,
As leaden minutes move by, I remain calm,
Imagining I really exist because of rhyme,
It alone allows me to insist I am, and I can defy time.
I cry out, I write therefore I am!

The Old Priest praises the love of his life, Christ

(*Frequently he's carried away by rare faith fervour*).

There is a shining lord of life:
As white as pearls upon a throat,
And strings of snow upon a tree;
As bright as diamonds on a hand,
The hand of Christ held out to me.

There is a golden lord of life:
As red as rubies on a sea,
Of glorious dresses worn for me,
By female angels out of eternity.

There is a folded cloth of life:
As dazzling as the morning light
Of God upon an opal sea;
The sea of life in Christ,
That I sail on to an eternity.

11

Yesterday I thought I saw the golden Christ
And everybody was closely pressed
Unto his pierced heart.

And all that was precious and the best
Of human life and art
Was held in his right hand.

An orb of light like crystal glass
Fell where his sacred glance fell
And even lit up hell itself.

And I cried, clasped to his breast:
"Let life be light, peace and grace,
In the embrace of the golden Christ!"

11

The love of God
Went deep into my soul,
So deep his love made me whole.

So that I began to glow
Inside, like a furnace stoked
Until fiery warm and alive.

He stole my being
And made it perfect
In his sight.

Refined in that furnace,
I was capable of intensely
Reflecting light.

Look at me, I, though
A poor creeping clod,
Am become the shining gold of God.

God so filled my soul,
In a moment at the Eucharist
So intense, I was defenceless.

Should I not then spread this grace?
Make all gold as I minister
To the lost, the old and the oppressed?

Is not this fire
I've received, unworthy though I be,
Given to set the world aflame with divinity?

Let me live in Christ,
In the fullness of that dream
Of universal spiritual Life, all that ought to be.

Bright as rainy spring blossoms,
Arising unseen,
Christ rainbows the earth with wisdom again and again.

Let those flowers
Of God's love, truth and beauty
Raise me to the glory of my own inner divinity.

Let eternal undying truth
Dispel the sterile emptiness
Of my otherwise empire of death.

Let my soul in God
Become a door, through which, a sacred thief,
All shining alive, he enters to steal away all sin and vice.

And let dark and the devil
Make way for his staying there
As I glow inside, intensely aware of his freeing care.

My life, my fullness!
My inner fire of fulfilment! God stiller
Of anxiety, infold me in elected silence.

Make me alive to your enduring charms
And give me the gift of prophecy,
That both pleases and alarms.

For when God has infolded me,
He had told me things
No man could on his own know.

How even the cold poles
Yes, all life, is wealth untold,
If seen aright as part of a divine plan.

In such times I marvel
Why he has chosen me to lie,
Like a child asleep on his breast.

Yet I know, like John,
How beautiful
It is to be so blessed.

The Old Man Praises Women

A woman presses roses
Into a book of pretty poems;
She arranges flowers,
Fragile as femininity,
As fleeting as beauty,
The old man said sadly.

Her bright dresses are frilled
Like those pressed petals,
And her lips are poppy red,
Calculated to awaken to desire
Even in the sleeping dead;
Rouge hides a pallid paleness,
And eye shadow is like the inside
Of opening pansies.

A woman finds babies adorable
Hers or others; once you discover women
They mother or smother you,
And yet are endearing, indispensable,
That needed other that bring completeness
To the frail, less capable, helpless male.

Women wait like tigers
Stalking that prey, yet pounce
Softly in silk,
Out of the dying day;
Tying a bright sandal
Over a white ankle,
Like a goddess of innocence at play.

Ah yes, I said, and surely women are much
More gentle and more full of beauty than us;
And if more of them were in charge of states,
Maybe the world would be a far better place.

Of Cats and Dogs

Cold are the stars in the sky tonight,
Cold as the shades of my lost delight.
The wailing winds in the wood tonight,
Tell of the dying of my light.
The tossing leaves in the tallest trees,
Tell of the failure of my muse.
The bitter storms from eastern lands,
Tell of my life as eroding sands,
In a timer not even verse withstands.

The shadows that gather on the lawn,
Tell of the coming time of doom,
And the death we all have to face alone.
The rise and rise of a mad red moon,
Tell of the apocalypse coming soon,
And the clouds that blot the stars and sun
Tell of the judgement day that's to come.

II

Then lo and behold a peaceful little dog
Appeared at my door, totally out of tune
With my melancholy mood of sad doom,
And also a furry little cat with pink eyes
Sat on the window sill like a wise Buddha.
They cheered me out of my doom huddle,

And I thought all of a sudden,
What would we do without cats and dogs
And all of the precious little pets we love.
We are so much in debt to the good Lord
For creating such things to keep us amused,
And be our companions in the darkest times.
And I thought if my cat died
I'd miss her so much I'd be inclined
To think animals have souls after all,
Or do they just absorb some of the soul
Of the ones they live with and adore?

Of Cats and Men

Today my cat
Brought a little mouse,
And proudly put it
At my feet,
Saying "look at the special treat
I bring, amn't I great?"
He didn't realise
That I wasn't a cat,
And didn't need a tiny
Plaything to hunt and kill.
For he let it go
And caught it again,
And looked proudly at me,
As if to say, "Amn't I a clever cat!"
Alas he was deceived, for I gave him no praise,
And I reflected on the fall,
And Adam and Eve's sin,
As I placed the mouse's dead bleeding body
In the refuse bin.

For those who love God

(More of the old man's grand faith fervour)

To those that love God
A restlessness in the bones
Drives them ever to his warm arms.

They come, numb with shock
Out of a dead world;
He rocks them to sleep.

To those that love God
Riches are rust, and the hype
Of the world hollow with vain dreams.

By streams crystal with song
Those that love God rinse their souls
With water that flows out of a fountain of wholeness.

Even tears brighten their faces;
They lie down in beds rich in silken truth and stretch
Their weak limbs on the rich divan of his healing teaching.

For there is no night
For those that love God;
Only the day when even pain is turned into prayer.

For to those that love God pain is never endlessly so.
There is fear, yes and suffering, as again and again
The darkness strikes at them:

Vulture-like with steely beaks seemingly
Stripping them to the bone;
Like Job they cry out strapped to a rock of torment.

But they are never really alone,
And such things are never forever;
The only thing that is so in the gentle love of the Father.

There is a recurrent rhythm,
And an insistent rhyme of salvation even in desolation;
Every indication of a final ecstatic destination.

The sky clears and sheer white clouds accumulate;
The sun climbs down to shine on them,
Heart-warming, soul-filling and mind-healing.

Gem on silver gem she shines out;
She wears her crown of peace;
There is ever an ageless mother
Of comfort and wisdom within for those who love God.

The Day my TV Blew Up

Today my TV blew up;
I suppose it became fed up
With me, and I with it,
Tired of my abuse of it;

And it of me;
As my immersion
In its superficial world
Ended, I cried "Whoopee"!

I took back my life,
And I was forever grateful
For the day
When my TV blew up.

The Angel of Peace (written during the Ukraine War)

And angel came to my door tonight
Fair as a star, bright
And innocent as a child's prayer,
With hair of gold and eyes of fire,
And wings as white as my window pane
On a snowy night, and his hands
Touched me soft as carded wool
On an Aran loom. "What brings thee
To my door dear angel?" I cried. He replied:
"I come alas, but with one word, doom,
It is coming as dark as the coldest winter night".

As he said this I seemed to hear drums beating,
As in a forest far away, drums of war
Again in Europe. "And how can I avert
This gathering doom?" I cried, "pray" he replied,
And believe again, stay close to the lord
And Mary, and pray, pray for peace, pray
Without cease day and night
That the light won't be completely blotted out
And I, the angel of peace, will finally triumph
Over the horrid demons of war, death and grief.

And in the eyes of one of the demons,
Who now appeared to me, I seemed to see
Streams of refugees and reams of broken homes,
And shattered cities and battered highways
To nowhere but blood and gore,
And floods of tanks and whines of missiles
I saw tearing the land apart. This can't go on,
I said, let the angel of peace reign like the sun,
Enter men's hearts, and still the guns

Of war forever, let him reign near and far,
So that our sons and daughters won't
Have to enlist in some bloody cause of power;
Or service of some brutal empire built by fire,
And senseless slaughter of the innocent child.

Then sadly the angel faded before my eyes
And I cried salt tears at his demise,
For he was angel of God, sent
To make me peaceful and wise,
And gentle as the eternal skies. And I surmised:
Man is proud and to gain his desires for power
Resorts to violence and war of every perverse kind;
By contrast the miracle is that God, the creative hub
Of the vast universe, is great enough for humble love.

Why again and again in sin I cried do people contrive
Endless wars against the clear will of the Lord's child?
The crucified witness of a gentle Jesus meek and mild.

The Still Point

"The still point of the turning world":
The poet saw it as a core of creativity,
The godly centre of the good and true,
And the fine divine core of me and you;
As of a sparkling diamond's inner core,
Or the pure glow of pearls in the light,
Or a moon that lights the darkest night.

"Suddenly I saw God in a point", Julian
Of Norwich said, a rare flash of insight
Into the causal core of all worldly life,
The Lord in everything bright and right.
The point of truth in white shining eyes
Of each innocent child or unspoilt youth,
Laughing faces, hearts of flowering truth.

The still point of a turning world unfurled
In the profounder depths of all our seeing,
In a core of peace in every authentic heart:
In science as Einstein's theory of relativity,
In a saint and hermit's holy inner serenity,
In all our birds of excited twittering flight,
In all the animals who cling fiercely to life
Defying demonic efforts to wipe them out.

"Suddenly I saw God in a point", life's point
In a baby growing from an initial little dot,
In an irrepressible child chuckling in his cot,
In a tree sprung from a tiny seed producing
Abundant leaves and fresh edible juicy fruit,
In all out fun or secret inner glee as we play,
In dot-like sun's warm promise of each day.

The heart meaning of every plant and flower,
The centre of sweet nectar that the bees seek,
The power of the atom's centre, the cell's core.
The centre of love in each lover's burning soul.
The selfless heart of a mother's tender caress,
Nature's inscape that visionary poets perceive,
A point of all things unique, their hidden grace.

The still point of the Master of life and eternity,
Contains the untold miracles of life that unfolds
In still centres of other turning worlds in space;
In galaxies of star-centred planetary complexity.
The warm centre suns round which they rotate,
Say the universe's divinely diverse and its point,
Like in Celtic motifs, spirals ever into an Infinite.

The Final Sleep

Lay me down in golden groves
Beside the waterfall,
Under the mountain of the lord
Where snipe and curlew call,
In a world where every creature is preserved,
And so the will of God, not only man, is served.

Lay me down by silver streams
Beside the lake of lethe,
Under the tower of gold,
Where angels white as light
Sing of the hundredfold,
Awaiting those who humbly served
The good of God, nature and humankind.

Lay me own in blessed fields
Beyond the reach of time,
By lime-white mansions of the Lord
In a perfect heavenly clime;
A land of song and poetic rhyme,
Where art is man's delight.
Where all prosper alike,
And all are made equal, as in God's sight.

Lay me down in the soundless place,
Beyond all jarring noise.
Where all are devout and wise,
And hear the poor man's cries,
And build the perfect race,
Beyond the chains of vice,
Filled with the peace of Christ.

Lay me down beyond all pain,
And let all darkness be in vain.
Let unbelief be the only crime.
Compose for me a symphony,
Of everything that's true and right,
And then forget I lived on a frail earth,
And tried in my poetry to pen its truth.

Then lay me down without a sound
In Cullen's ancient and holy ground.

After Matisse

Let's escape a world of colourless drab design,
I want the reader's spirit to be one with mine
In a voyage to the forest of time beyond time:
Let them sit with me drinking old ruby wine
Amid the colours of the heart, let's redesign
Reality as a finer tapestry of colour and line.

There doors opens and I step onto a silver floor,
Embossed with diamonds and opals of desire,
And panels of red and yellow enamel fire;
And vivid backgrounds of bright vermilion,
And whirling gyres of prancing-pony carousels.

My rime expands: in colour's hands I hold up
Blue jade birds, and lions of polished gold,
And leopards with brown and fawn spots,
And fabulous flocks of fairground-hued butterflies,
Fluttering onto a rain-forest's amber autumn floor.

The petals of multi-coloured flowers
Blow around me without a sound,
As I stain like Matisse a light green glow
Of fronds on panels of the chapel door,
Exploded and set off by deep purple;
The violet kingship robes of heaven's king,
Seated on a red throne of velvet poetic song.

Though I go there bowed and old,
When a tree is about to die,
Like Matisse, that's when it produces the best fruit.
So I leave as my legacy the poetry beyond death:
Like the Mona Lisa as smiling and mysterious
As a final banquet of the blessed in white robes,
Let colour and winged words be my hundredfold.

Like the chapel background of forms Matisse amassed,
May I earn my rest by painting God's glory as a priest.
Like Houdini let me escape the world's chains, be blest
By bright tints and shades to defy Satan's colourless ways.
In words let me show off life's glory like a peacock's tail,
And soar like Matisse through the bars of hell's drab jail.

Easter in Jerusalem (orthodox)

Converted from coldness
The old things fold up
Became faceless memories.
I hold up icons
I never knew before.
Kiss jewel-encrusted
Crosses. Carry gold
Incense-dispensers, read
Silver-covered missals
Embossed with moulded madonnas
And robed Christ-childs
In embroidered copes
Wearing crowns
Studded with diamonds
I walk among my former fears
That kiss my opal rings
And sing alleluias
In shrill ecstatic voices.
Cowered at the back
Of the congregation, my old
Voices no longer beckon
But are washed away by the carved crosses
De... ... in stone processions

Suffering

"Life is a vale of soul making" – Keats

There is no greatness without suffering,
The old man said, after a time of grief and pain
He lay, my captain muse, *"Fallen, cold and dead"*.
I now know that when we are too content
A slow poison eats away our souls, he continued;
We forget God and burrow dark holes like moles
Into the clay depths of pale malnourished souls.

We never know the character growth that comes
From going through every suffering and sorrow,
And rising above it to faith in the very marrow bone;
Knowing God is no Sugar Daddy ruling puppet souls;
Intervention would negate a greater good, our freedom,
And the freedom of a world that with man fell from Eden;

No! Life's a necessary struggle, but not one without gain;
The soul deepening in God forged by life's essential pain.

As the Irish folk song says:
"The weight upon your shoulders
Will make you a stronger man".

The Mystery of Space

Again and again I would lay me down
In grass as sweet as may meadows;
And look up at the evening sky and say:
Let all my days be unrestricted space;
Let my pleasures be pure and bright
As shining depthless heavenly lights.

For up there space is endless surprises;
Let me seek the vast limitless horizons
Of the soul up there, final blue serenity,
Ageless galaxies of a universal divinity;

Man is mad, a world of space watches
As he rants and raves to grave and gory
Destruction; as his time plays itself out
Billions of galaxies remain without tears.

So I sing of that bright spangled universe's
Matchless immensity of space and matter,
Its high silver wealth should make us wise:
Let's be humble beside those huge designs!

O blue and precious rose of high resolution!
O untroubled untarnished deep above us!
Let you never finish your course through
Timeless time's untouched roads of space!

Sing on! Let your suns always splash fire,
Sprout light! Let them diamond the night
As our planet gradually dies; sparkle high
Above us, fierce lamps of love, and praise!
And perfection that existed long before us!
And will exist long after doors close on us.

Fire on ageless meteorites, you black holes,
You hold both heaven and hell in your fold!
Be dazzling delight years to me and mirrors
Of God's highway in space's immense infinity!
Far above all our reductive emblems of Deity.

For Calvary's greater than space's immensity.

Patterns of Outer and Inner Space

The Poet discovers the magic of Colour in Patterns

Lay me down finally
In golden groves
Beside the silent sea,
Where colours and designs
Speak to me,
Of the glories of eternity.

For the colours of life
Are glorious to behold:
The emerald of fields;
The aquamarine of the sky;
The red rose in gardens of repose;
The purple of pomp
And the orange of the lamp
We lived by at night
Before electric light;
The limp white of lilies;
The pale puce of grape juice;
We drink ruby wine.

The dark of blackberries
We picked in quarries;
The grey of rabbits
We caught in snares;
The silver of rivers
Filled with blue skies and snow clouds;
The multi-colours of fluttering butterflies
Among the many-hued meadow flowers;
Deep red poppies like ladies lips,
And the glistening yellow of buttercups;
Shy violets hiding in ditches,
And the showy gold of furze;

The pinkish white of blackthorn blossoms,
And the purple of loganberries;
The muted red of haws,
And the deep purple of sloes;
The flashing green and silver of trout
Darting about in deep dark river pools.

Colours are life's wealth
As every artist knows,
They gladden the heart
When everything else fails.
Simply laid down they don't seem much,
But put in patterns
They astonish and delight;
As the impressionists knew
Intoxicated by the fascination
Of colours that breathed magic,
And seemed every changing and new,
Infinitely varied and full of fabulous delight,
When captured in ceaselessly changing light.

The Dark Tower (written in Palestine during the Intifada)

"Childe Roland to the Dark Tower Came" – The Song of Roland.

Someone inserted war and strife
Into the wheel of people's colourful pilgrim life;
It was the evil one: that thief of souls
Was envious of human happiness
In a holy garden without violence;

So the god of war was loosed even in a holy land;
Now what people or place is safe from his cruel hand?
For man's thirst persists for domination and power,
So he continually serves the lord of the dark tower;
We can only cry, God help us all! We can only call
On the Prince of Peace who walked these streets:
O Grant us the graces needed to defeat the vile beast!

Only the Prince of Peace can defeat that dark lord,
Satan that fallen star, who having descended
Far into the abyss, still seeks to quench the light
He cannot bear; he wants to turn humans to death,
And sow endless darkness and suffering on earth.

He, aided by arrogant empires, in desire for power
Carries history to bloody towers of endless wars;
Usually justified by webs of warmongering words;
Our era saw Satan carry many to hell in tanks and planes,
Down to vast underworld gulags of torture, grief and pain;

Surely it is time to cease! To say stop, no more!
Let's follow instead blessed peacemakers who share
The gentle mission of the opposite good lord!
It's sad that in a lust for power, in every single year,
Men still promote and justify all sorts of senseless wars;
Not learning from history, we live it over and over forever.

O Follow the Christmas message "*goodwill* among men",
Like the soldiers did in 1916: let's dig up trench lines;
We know we must do so; all that we need is a *will* to defeat
The evil ones designs; if we had but that firm will, peace
Would've come long ago: know we can make wars cease!
All we need's good will, rejection of every lust for power,
So future Childe Rolands won't languish in the dark tower.

II

The Bethlehem skyline
Blisters in the summer sun;
Clouds of woolly wishes
Never fully understood,
Are set within my wine glass,
To marinate, as I painfully
Contemplate, Beit Sahour
Under curfew, and a soldier
Beating an innocent boy
With a machine-gun butt;
The god of war is alive
Here, before my dazed eyes.
That frail child had come,
Through no fault of his own,
To be beaten down and imprisoned
Every day in the dark tower of war;

O lock up torture doors of all dark towers today!
I cried, let children be free to enjoy peace, to play!

Conversion

I saw the pale light of the sun
Illuminating the cloisters where the nuns
Walked two by two, beads rattling
Skirts swishing, women prattling
At recreation; and I saw someone run
In the convent gate, with a smattering
In English: "he has a gun, a gun" they scream.

At the door stood the intruder, laughing:
"Give me all you have and more", he began muttering.
Then out of the terrified virgin throng, an old nun
Stepped forward and said: "young man, we have alas,
No money to give you, but we can give you God's peace".

Now a servant of God, stays in cloister with the nuns,
He kneels and prays, it's that man, now without guns.

Peace on Earth

There will be no peace on earth
The old man said
Until there is peace in each human heart
In union with the Prince of Peace:
I sat back waiting to be bored
By another lengthy monologue
Of other-world sermonising,
Yet, resting his case, he was silent;

I was forced thereby to see
The simple logic of his argument:
If peace is in each human heart
Then peace will be everywhere,
Without fail, war is gone forever.

There is no war, he went on, no sin
In the Buddhist or Christian convent,
Established to cultivate peace within.

Fleeing a Troubled World

Do not let the world
Destroy you peace
The old man continued:
By now I was thoroughly fed up
With the repeated sermonic theme,
Though like the Ancient Mariner
I was caught up in his narrative as in a dream.

Do not let the world
Destroy your peace, my child!
So much that it does
Disturbs me, disturbs you;
Do not let the world indoctrinate you
And destroy your peace;
Be away from it all; you must cease
From buying, crying and striving
At the world's beck and call;

Do not let the world
Destroy your peace:
Though all that you love
Crumbles around you,
Release the pent-up pain
In the power of the pen;
And find peace within!

Do not let the world
Destroy your peace:
Though it hold you
In a vice of vice;
And in the media that is its voice;
Do not let the world destroy your peace;

Remember God was crucified
By the corrupt world he dared to criticise;
Yet even on the cross beside violent thieves,
He refused to let cruel rulers or autocratic priests,
Destroy the gentleness of his divine heart of peace.
Ah, my child, be like him!
Do not let worldly violence destroy your inner peace.

Away from the Media

Turn away from the media
The old man said,
And you will be freer inside:
Be free from the ideologies and prejudices
That would make you a cipher, he went on,
Helplessly floating in its dominating tide;

Be original and set all that conditioning aside:
All those words and images that might
Make us buy what we do not want or need;
All those ads and fads and addictive mechanical
Games and toys that would make everyone
The same cipher, playing the same violent games;

Turn away from the media and find time
To be at peace with oneself: time to think
And contemplate and pray; time to walk
With nature every day; time to live with one's
Hands in the clay out of which we were made;

Turn away from the media and try to be a free
Son or daughter of the stars: set the imagination
Free from all mind-conditioning prison bars;
All that makes of life a jailhouse abode for the soul;

Turn away from the media and discover
Your own greater inner freedom and heart gold!
Turn away from the media and be unsoiled,
Like in the free skies of the innocent unfettered child;
Turn away from the media and be unsold merchandise.

In Dream Anthony the Hermit speaks to me

"Unto a desert go", a voice in my hungry heart said;
I was glad to obey; I was so tired of the Roman state
I lived in; it was corrupt, immoral in so many ways;

I did not want to let that world
Destroy the inner peace I yearned for
And was gradually building up in Christ;
It was like your island retreat, poet,
Your escape to the fringe of the far west;

There in the desert I built my retreat,
My concave cells of simplest design;
Others, kind souls, brought me food and wine
Though I did not ask for what they supplied;
Gradually more alienated faithful fled to my side.

They asked for my prayers and advice, and young men
And women tired of the world and its ways came to stay
With me and build similar cell homes; we even organised
A central chapel and dining hall for those hosts of saints;
These eager souls needed to live a worthwhile holy life
Rather than being fodder for the world's ways and wars;

I wish people would choose a similar wise way today;
To come apart and pray, to cast off worldly chains of clay;
I said to the holy hermit as his image faded from my view.
And I awoke to the fading light on a dreary rainy Irish day.

Reason for a Rhyme

I drew from out
My soul in time
An ageless reason for a rhyme,
The Lord within
My soul in time;
For always his presence
In my heart,
Makes sweet
The beauty of my art,
Turning my words into a door
That opens into forever more.

For the soul knows more
Than the mind can hold:
Golden thoughts and dreams,
From untold
Realms of space within,
Beyond thought and beyond sin;

The soul knows more
Than the mind can hold:
There wells up
From a well within
Fountains of faith,
And intuitive truth;

The soul sees more
Than the mind can seize;
Angel foam breaking on rocks of soul seas,
And the fiery cloak of God in falling leaves;

The soul feels more
Than the heart can feel;
Joys and tears and vast despairs,
Dark nights and morning inspires;

The soul knows more
Than the mind can hold,
Glimpses from the heavenly home
It came from and would return to:
Archangels with wings of light;
And saints with haloes of gold,
Righting a world too harsh or cold;

The soul know more
Than the mind can hold;
The mind tries to give
Form to what the soul conceives,
And it succeeds only on its knees.

A Blue Heaven

The world vibrates
with the colours of life.
Even when we are old
Something within us
is still young & alive.
The world that vibrates eternal
with the colours of life
of which my soul is a part
as every
deep desires

The kernel of man
is the eternal
wonders from the vernal
forest of infused light
Where all is pure
& clean & bright
Where woods are green
& all is untouched delight
The kernel of man
is the eternal land
where birds sing
& no creature is in danger
of being wiped out
But all is as it was at beginning
Innocent, fair & shining

The Road

The road runs far away
Into the grey land of nothingness.
The road runs always
Further than we can follow;
Uphill and down hollow
It knows no rest.
The best falter
That try to trace its route
To the end of the rainbow,
The apex of thought and truth
In the blue of the everlasting night.

They are gone
But the road runs on.
The stones that pave it
Are men and women's bones,
For the road does not even begin
To consider what humanity means.

The road leans
Neither to the left or right.
It rolls through another day, another night,
Another year, decade, century,
It is all the same.
Men fight or are at peace,
Men build or break down,
Men laugh or cry,
Men live or die,
The road sees all, and passes on.
It knows everything and nothing
For the road is time and nothing
Except maybe this rhyme
Will outlive the road of time.

Then let it roll on!
We follow for a while,
And then falter and are gone.
We fall by its earthen side.
Others carry on.
They cover us and pass by,
Maybe with a momentary tear or sigh.
That is all.
The road carries them
On to the same end,
Though they know and
Do not know it.
All individual things are,
And are not in the long run.
Yet the road of life
Rolls around every bend we invent,
And never comes to an end.

The Moon

Why does the moon
Light up our hearts,
On dark nights
When we are alone?
Why does it not disturb
With its cold silver music?
Why is its song so sweet?
Bringing magical imaginations
Flowing into the brain?
Why is the moon then
Like a lost child holding out
His white helpless hands to us?
Pathetic, appealing, full of trust!

Why is the moon like a mirror
Of all our hopes? Lighting up the darkness
We grope in, yes like all our optimisms
Our absurd dreams; at times like that
I feel I could worship the yellow disc
Gleaming out of vast blue space,
Out of the sky's mindless emptiness
It shows us a strange mystical face.

Why is the moon so comforting?
I am up here watching over you,
It seems to say, when life seems grey.
It is one of the brighter enduring things
Like the sun or the stars,
Or the eyes of God himself observing us
From the immense heavens.
Why is the moon manly, brisk bracing
Erasing all the memories of the day
In one sweep of silken rays?

Ah, songster of the night, majestic moon!
Adored by poets and lovers, stay always above us!
Beaming over the world always, despite our sicknesses
You remain the same, we look up to you, don't let us down!

II

We went to the moon,
But our manned flights
Stopped there;
When will we explore
The universe to its end?

Or is it not linear,
Like we once thought the earth,
But cyclical, ever cycling
Back on itself;
Spiralling to infinity,
From which the moon came,
In a universe that's endless cyclical time.

The Drug of Poetry

Poetry is like a drug:
You cannot leave off;
Once you have begun
It drags you along,
Day after day,
Night after night,
In pursuit of the youth
And freshness
That is to write.

Always the next poem
Will be better;
Always what you've written,
Looking back,
Seems the work of a hack;
You break your back,
And see nothing for it
But a stone clod of poems,
Groping and groaning
Their way to the seamless stars.

The Maze of Evil

The empire of evil never sleeps
In the darkness of nothingness,
A dreadful eternal nightmare in life,
The empire of evil never sleeps.

In a world that endlessly crucifies
The vulnerable the poor and the weak,
The empire of evil never sleeps.

In an earth that kills faith and saving grace
In a drip drip of inner death in life,
The empire of evil never sleeps.

In the streets of ragged homeless children,
The empire of evil never sleeps.

In the grimy back ways of boys
And girls as forced work or sex slaves,
The empire of evil never sleeps.

In the trenches of killing fields
Flowing with blood and poison gas,
The mass graves of boys without names,
The empire of evil never sleeps.

In the clinics where,
The sworn to save life doctors kill,
The empire of evil never sleeps.

In the camps and gulags of the mad
Ideologies of our ages, and the droppers
Of atomic bombs or agents oranges,
The empire of evil never sleeps.

But the sad thing is that even when soaked in blood
It's often portrayed as an empire of good;
The philosopher was right, men decide what they want
According to their dark desires, and then think up
Plausible ideologies to justify their corrupt choices.
Is that the reason why the empire of evil never sleeps?

The Maze of Good and Evil

The Proverbs of the Old Man

Yesterday the old man died
And by his bed I found these scribbles
From the wisdom he'd acquired in life.

He that sows in lies
Shall not lack a harvest
But it will be a harvest of death
He who sows in truth
Will not lack a harvest
But it will be a harvest of eternal youth

He who sows in vice
Will not lack a harvest
But it will be a harvest of hell

He who sows in virtue
Will not lack a harvest
But it will be a harvest of paradise

What we sow of good or ill
While on earth, we will reap
As our harvest for all eternity

Every good deed we do in life
Will echo throughout eternity

Every evil deed we do in life
Will echo throughout eternity

The lies of the false can influence us
As much as the truths of the wise

Only the wisdom of life's true prophets
Endures the reaping of time's knife

What is sown in laughter
We will reap in joy ever after

What is sown in sorrow
Will lead to a leaden tomorrow

What is sown in prayer
We will harvest in the Lord's care

What is sown in blasphemy
Will be harvested in perversity

What is sown too soon
Will be harvested too soon

What is sown too late
Will never come into the light

What is sown in insight
Will be harvested in wisdom

What is sown in foolishness
Will be harvested in illusion

What is sown in senselessness
Will be harvested in chaos

What is lost through love in time
Will be gained in eternity

The essence of success
Is prudent persistence

The essence of failure
Is the refusal to deal with detail

The muse is strange
He speaks the truth
Though he doesn't realise he does so

II

No one heals himself
By wounding another person
No one fails to heal himself
In healing another person

No one fails to love himself
In loving another person

No one ever fails to love others
If he truly loves God

No one who ever truly
Loves the true God
Ever fails to do immense good

Only in God is the greatness
Of humanity understood

My secret soul
Which I reveal to you
Stands against the cruel ways
Of the world, like a wall

Time move on
And what will we leave behind
A blot or a blossom
Upon the page of time?

What is art from the heart understood
But an open doorway to immortal good

The greatest victories
Are the victories we gain
Over our baser self

The greatest freedom
Is in doing what is right
Regardless of the cost
The greatest heroes of our era
Have done just that

As Coleridge knew
The greatest art
Is to reveal deep down
Below the heart
And nature's mysteries
The invisible soul of life
And God that is its source

The emptiness of life
And the suffering of being
Makes me constantly quest
For what I cannot achieve

Further wise words of the dying Old Man

Words delight the heart,
And art delights the mind.
Truth brings back our youth,
And doing right keeps us pure inside.
Faith nurtures the soul,
And needs a church to keep it alive.
Belief is a spring leaf,
And a blossom that never dies.
Song gives the person wings,
And verse satisfies an inner thirst.
Rhyme is the measure of time,
And rhythm is the cosmic hymn.
Love is a flower from above,
And richer than a treasure trove.
Friendship is the ship of humanity,
That carries it to fair warm shores.
Charity for the lost and the poor,
Is the roadway to heaven's door.
Trust is our souls only must,
If we're to have any faith at all.
Hope is a dangling rope,
By which we climb heaven's castle wall.
Duty is the fruit of authenticity,
And leads on to working felicity.
Desire is the fire in the belly,
That leads to fruitful sexual activity.
Fatherhood is a blessed role,
And motherhood is the best role of all.
The fatherhood and motherhood of God
Is the basis of every creative good.

Naming God

What shall I call you? Lord,
King, Yahweh, Adonai, Kairos?
Almighty father, Christ, Jesus?
Everything that ever is or could be?

Shall I call you Trinity or Mary?
Or Saviour, Providence or perfection?
Or all excellence? Shall I call you Abba?
Or Absolute, or Divine Truth?
Or is there anything I can really say
About you, except that you are deity?
Are all my categories unsatisfactory?
Except Love, the heart of the Trinity.

Shall I call you Spirit or Ghost?
Or God or Mother? Or are you
Far too other, too demanding
For my pathetic understanding?

Can I grasp you by will alone?
Or can my imagination rise
To some sensational vision,
That will see the beauty of your visage?
Your untold brightness of being?
An intense light it's death to see.
Despite my sinfulness, can I grasp in insight
Your immense holiness? Or is that vision
Wholly beyond my poor inner eyesight?

I'm partly made in your image
And did you not appear in Christ?
Can I see you there? Or is his grandeur
Also too infinite for my grasping hands?

One thing alone is sure:
I shall see you and know you
No sandman, in that other land
Where I trust you will bring me at last,
To know you and be with you everlastingly.
For the moment the best I can do
Is to love you as unlimitedly as I can,
And find you in the deep prayer of the heart.
Where I can name you as my life and my art.

Achill

Where better to pen poems of natural wonders
Than in Achill on the edge of the western world?
There I stand on cliffs washed by seas as emerald
As stony fields under grey skies above a blue bay.

By bobbing fish boats on this day of July 1998,
Busy sheep cropping on the side of steep cliffs
Bleat at me, as I compose poems by towering crags
Gutted by grey granite and old sandstone caves.

In this abode of stones, I stand silent and alone,
Dreaming of a hermitage hewn from its bones.
Above me gulls scream to disturb my streams
Of idyllic dreams; visions thrive in this island.

It is made of poetry! So it is my spiritual home,
As are the ever-washing waves of its golden shore.
Here I'm still near to the Lord, having moved here
From Knock's chapels of mystic Marian devotions.

There I wished I could stay in prayer forever
(For God, Mary and living angels were there),
In rich flowering grounds and by visionary altars,
I sketched, in notebooks, Knock's mystic features.

Achill extends that pilgrimage, though the idyll
Is invaded by holiday homes and tourist bus loads.
Standing by snowy spray wearing an Aran sweater
And on my neck a Celtic cross, I praise the creator.

And dream of staying in a simple parish like this,
To serve God, write and love in the spirit of monks
Who lived here in splendid isolation for many years,
And built monasteries to praise a God so easy to find

Amid wild blowing bog-cotton sea-borne storms,
And fogs, and the thrill of the oceans also within
Beyond death, and vain profit, and sin, listening
To winds sighing as they chanted sacred psalms.

Achill II

Monks gone, on the golden beach I see a dead
Black-backed gull, crumpled up under its wide
Wings like a sleeping child in death. I wonder
Why he died? I fear it wasn't just natural causes.

More likely some modern chemical man-made
Concoction had burned his free wild heart away.
I remember, only yesterday, seeing in the sea
A large black mackerel swimming nonchalantly,

Obviously saved by the sea. He had survived
Close to the pier, in and out of tangled clumps
Of auburn Achill sea-weed, like fingers through
One's hair, or a poet seeking a home of the free.

Now as I watch by great furrowed cliffs, as black
As the gills of old mushrooms, a tiny twittering
Bird sweeps by me and lands on the fearful edge
Of a sheer fall, wall after wall of death below him.

By washing sounds of eternal seas; that bird is me
Living among the rocks pinks and white clumps
Of thrift in a cave hewn out of Achill's hill heights,
I'd delight day in day out in soul-bird songs of light.

And in solitude complete my soul island pilgrimage.
Living among windy, rainy and wondrously green
Fields of a retreat where the breezes breed serenity
And tidal rhythms are as restful as a child's lullaby

Too gentle to be true? I hear a tourist bustling by
Say: playing the golf last week we were drenched:
Rain is all he remembers, not wild beauty all about;
That only the poet and lover of the isles really sees,

A feast of timeless island beauty fine in any weather,
Raising the heart and the soul to praise of the creator
Of these shores of grandeur by glorious western seas,
That the pure in heart can see as signs of divine light!
Beauty alive in any weather to those open to its truth.

The coat

For a long time in my life
I thought myself alone,
Drifting without meaning
In a world cold as stone;
A man only of frail flesh
And bone, with despair as a wife.

Now I know that is not so,
For alone in prayer I heard the spirit say:
There is one who knows you
Who is constantly with you, Con.
Someone to whom you can hold on to
Confidently, Con, even when life itself is gone.

Someone who takes you for what you are;
Someone who holds your hand,
Keeps you from being put upon by the world;
Someone who cares and bears you up,
Lest you dash your foot against a stone;
It is Christ I talk of Con, and your heavenly home.
Cornelius, Con, Corny, take hold of God
Like a woolly coat, to protect you against the cold.
Over the shirt of the spirit and the pants of Christ
Put on your overcoat of God glorious blessedness,
And sink in its woolly folds in mind and soul rest.

It will warm you forever, Con; leave you never,
It will keep you safe in the wild fields of life,
As you walk the cold earth on the way to paradise,
A pale pilgrim, it will keep you safe from icy vice.

I the spirit promise it, I guarantee the coat's quality Con;
Wear it in all worldly snow and frost until I come at last.
I am Christ, wear my coat and it will
Comfort you in life's ups and downs,
And finally clothe you forever in heaven's home, Con.

I answered that I would and would not be afraid.
I would put it over me and live in its woolly folds;
I would let it shelter me, and never let it be sold
For a mess of pottage, or vain useless worldly gold;
I would wear forever the warm embroidered coat of Christ
To clothe my heart, my art and my soul until I'm at rest,
Until I put on a coat of many colours among the blessed.

The Coat of Many Colours

I

More than ~~that~~ I do not know.
More, than falling rain, or drifting
                        snow.
More than flowers in a May field.
More than the joy ~~that~~ reflection yields.

More than love and more
                than law
More than life sweetness somehow
My adherence to the Word
leads me into broad bright
                ways
Lights up all my nights
                and my days.

More than madness and more
                than pain
More than all the thoughts
That cluster in my brain
More than all the memories that
        light my lonely way

More than a good book or a
        powerful play
The Lord's words thunder in
                my soul
Expanding my being making

Dreams

I am amazed at what dreams we saw,
My soul and I,
When, on pages untouched
And white as snow,
We wrote the poems, given to us
From whence we did not know.

O dreams make or break me!
Like kneaded dough,
Make me into a loaf
For the lord of life
And bake me in the furnace
Of the world's pain and strife.

O dreams make me a knife!
Let you saw through,
Or cut away the veils
That obscures life's glory and delight.

O dreams make me fit
To speak of marble halls!
And crystal bowls,
And inlaid azure floors,
In the high heavens,
Beyond all nights of the soul.

Show me doors of beaten bronze,
Opening unto heavenly homes,
And silver flowers of the moon,
Lighting away all my inner glooms;
And banishing the blue of my lonely nights,
In golden blossoms of God's dawning lights.

On wings of dreams I would be gone!
To pick the apples of the sun,
And gather the red rosebuds of June.
For white and high and evermore
Are the dreams that take my soul and I
To happy highlands and cloudless skies.
Knowing true art is incapable of telling lies.

And let these best blessed dreams of Home
Raise up my pale bones to heaven's throne,
When I'm just a pile of dust beneath a stone.

The Visionary

Though I have to suffer for my Art
Who but the martyr can know
Xt's ~~Sacred~~ Heart

And since of the pure bright
Heart of Xt is the only
Sure light in a cold world
Beyond the unfolding dance of death
What can ~~this~~ but appear
in pure Heart-blood art
That sure a untold delight
For there is no other well against the NIGHT
And if I build that well
Brick on brick, word on word
design on design
well it not be a saving light
forever for the human mind
for it is not mine, but the well
against death of the immortal Xt
And I'm just a dot in that vast
design
Without the passion of the ~~...~~

And if the BIRDS of eternal thought
peek out of that cauldron
of lines then ~~...~~ a billionth
of the ~~...~~ of Xt ~~...~~

Mouse Fable

A mouse once lived
In a castle tower,
Guarded by demons
Hour by hour.
And thought to himself
How can I escape?
For Satan holds
The keys of the gate.
Then he thought he heard,
In his tiny brain,
The echo of this
Profound refrain:
Pray to the Lord
It will not be in vain.
He prayed, this little miserable mouse,
And down fell devils, and gate, and house.
The mouse, in gratitude,
Scampered away,
On his saintly relics
Revered today.

On Mary Miles Going Away

You beguiled me
With you smiling eyes,
My pretty neighbour
Mary Miles.

You beguiled me
With your flowing hair,
As fair and bright
As the summer hours,
We spent discussing
Our gardens and flowers,
A passion for nature
Both of us shared.

You moved away,
And I was in tears.
But I'll ever remember
Your warmth and smiles,
My ex-next-door angel,
Mary Miles.

II

Golden were the hours
We shared, drinking lemonade
Under a rose bower shade,
That scented the smiles
You gave me, and I gave you,
My gentle neighbour Mary Miles.
Silver were the moonlit nights,
We sat on the veranda,
Sipping old ripe wine,
That enlivened the smiles
You gave me, Mary Miles.
The smiles are gone,
But in memory you
Are always by my side,
I'm never alone,
Though you're now under a stone.
I still dwell in the depths
Of deep alive brown eyes,
Gazing in mine,
And the soft red kisses
You gave my soul for while,
My lovely neighbour,
Mary Miles.

The Old Man and Mary Miles —Ghosts of my Imagination

Like the old man, Mary Miles
You never existed,
Yet I still miss
Your wonderful kisses,
Maybe because I am mad,
And want so badly
That which I never had.

Mary Miles you still
Sit in the corner of my garden smiling,
Your amber eyes shining,
And your hair like the weeping willow
Hanging down over my shoulders,
Enveloping me in tresses like silken flowers.
Ah, how I weep for all that I felt of beauty with you,
That never existed and is now with me forever true!

The old man and Mary Miles
Never existed and yet are more real to me
Than twisted tales of famine, war and disease
On the radio and TV. That's reality,
But is it the reality we want to see and be?
I write to create the world God wants us
To create and live in. That we can do
If we but will it, for where there is will
There is a way; we don't have to live
Always in world of brutal bloody strife
And poison-gas clay slime underfoot.

The old man and Mary Miles never existed,
Yet they were more real to me
Than the grim news on Radio and TV.
Art's beauty is real, cruel reality is unreality.

So let's create the world we want to live in
Through art! And then bring it into being,
For in art we can create any world we want,
And so inspire others to live from the heart.

For as Saussure says, all reality anyway
Is a construct, let the ideal be our construct,
Art our doorway to a freer and fairer earth.

Not Afraid to Love

Do not be afraid to love,
The saintly old priest said,
Lacking love the church will be lost,
And the world will crumble into dust.

Do not be afraid to love,
The wise old priest said,
Without love the heart will shrivel,
And the spirit will tumble into hell,
The icy depths of life's hateful well.

Never decide to hate,
The old holy priest said,
For in the darkness of hate
Your inner light will slowly go out.

Do not be lost, wandering
Among the bare winter forests of hate,
For there you will never hear the birds
Of morning singing of life's delights.

Decide to love and you'll be loved,
The kind old priest said,
And you will have many soul mates
Waiting for you in the great halls above.

Heaven, a warm timeless home,
Is for kindly loving hearts alone.
For the main gain of living
Is the glorious pain of loving.

After the Apocalypse

It was a fine autumn:
It was the first time
I noticed the leaves falling;
And how beautiful they were;
Their colours recalling,
The autumns we knew
When we were young and innocent;
All red and orange and brown,
Tumbling down in quiet
Misty gentle weather,
In tune with nature's music
Of birds bringing summer's magic.

And chestnuts strewing the floor;
And old nests exposed
On the defoliating trees;
And I thought sadly, I have not seen
The world's beauty even in winter until now?
Maybe the Maya apocalypse was right,
A new more spiritual age is on the way,
After the old one is swept away.

When I can learn to see again
And pray and play,
And write poems of glory,
Without being weighed down with cares;
And speak warm words to those around me,
From love is the glory of the alive soul,
Before winter comes and the earth
Finally grows cold and dead as a stone.

And I resolved to write poems about
Beauty alone from now on;
To stir the heart to healing song,
Before I passed along
Like lovely autumn leaves;
To leave something behind,
Before I grow blind
And deaf and dumb
To the beauty of the world,
And the glory of the people I loved.

Visions of the New Jerusalem

One night in a vision of delight,
After I'd gone to sleep pale and distraught,
An angel opened for me a golden door of truth.
And light from the heavenly transcendent
Floor of faith, shone like the radiance
From a pearl necklace on the throat of Lady Charity,
Mother Mary; suddenly all my paleness faded
To the golden glow of hope and life fully restored.

Like a diadem on the head of maiden life in Christ,
I saw my grey bones turn into living ones,
And my ancient grey locks into fair festoons of hair
Falling over shoulders bare and bright,
As in the very flower of golden youth;
Then a voice said, this is you in a prime body
Alive at the final resurrection of those worthy.

And raised up around me I saw billions of holy souls,
Putting on perfect bodies that shone with the glory
Of the eternal blessed saints, that were now like God.
Out of the bejewelled floor of this New Jerusalem,
Fair as a perfect youthful bride on the wedding day,
There shone the light of a thousand stars,
Out of the blue robe of an eternal night become day.

And I heard Michael in dazzling array, say:
Now is all the world's pain become the sunshine
Of a perfect paradise regained, joy beyond imagining.
There stainless angels with opal wings wandered,
Singing forever the purest and fairest eternal hymns.

Then a great gong sounded and along the pearly floor
Of forever more a stream flowed of old mature
Red wine, and gin, and whiskey galore, that all drank
From, of whatever they wished, and sat down to dine
At the great banquet of the just beyond the famine of time.

And they then paired off into glorious kissing couples,
Restored as it were to their wedding day on earth,
Arrayed with golden rings and ruby jewels,
And rare pearl necklaces that would never fade away;
They played in a fair gardens of every colour flower
And juicy fruit, and I saw there fine passionate youth
Playing football or whatever sport they favoured on earth,
On fields by mansions prepared for them from all time,
As kindly fathers and mothers watched with loving care.

The clime was a sunny one with soft sparkling showers
To keep everything constantly fresh, green and fruitful.
And I saw storytellers and poets telling tales to enthralled
Throngs, and skilled musicians playing classical and pop
Melodies and tuneful voices singing every sort of fine song.

As all became weary, another great gong was sounded,
And all went into lavish rooms and lay on soft beds,
To sleep the all-refreshing sleep of God's holy ones.
It had become night, but not a night dark as of lost demons
But the clear night of the blessed, and the stars over them
Sparkled like dazzling diamonds on the throat of heaven.
Ah here at last I cried are my heart wishes! And my soul's
Fullness of longed for eternal truth, right and inner delight.

I awoke to find myself all alone on a cold grey rainy night.

Marija of Medjagorje
As you gaze at Mary's glory
And her love profound
Sound in our souls
Her beautiful songs
That we may melt in God's arms
And all wrong divine
[...] into [...]

Let us also see Her face
Mother of all life & grace deepest
And queen of our hearts
The feminine in God we have
many rejected, but catholics protected
but to bring balance to our belief
Stars reel around you
Marija, for a mother of light is here
They steal into your hair
In God, your heart is a heart of fire
The vivgin angels

Around you never tire praising
their Lord
They kneel in prayer
I seem to hear the angels sing within to
Core of everything
And more before Mary

Their Mother & yours.

We cannot see them
But know they are there
Numerous angels
from the throne of God
Sent with Mary
To care for us   who never
                        cease to
They are everywhere. →
OUR [...] angels of God's love & [...]

The New Church

Having discussed all we could invent,
The old man fell back on the bed, spent,
But later, revived, he brought up this theme at length.
Set aside a cold moralising we inherited from
Reformation Platonism, Renaissance Patriarchy,
That banned Mary and incarnational Christianity.

Set aside that inhumane mind and again find
The human one of gentle Jesus meek and mild.
Return to trust and God's humble people heed;
Let's obey what they tell us they want and need.

Let the God of gentle love be the church's true face,
So searching lost souls may find in it their home place.
And the poorest of the poor find in it succour and rest;
For down in the dust with Christ the church's at its best.

Only thus can it do its duty, serve its divine call,
To help humanity accept its glory, heaven's will.

The Will, the Key to Everything

The key to everything is the will, the old man said,
As he taught me from grand lands of the holy dead:

The will to life or the will to death
The will to lies or the will to truth
The will to peace of the will to war
The will to love or the will to hate
The will to beauty or the will to ugliness
The will to virtue or the will to vice
The will to family or the will to self
The will to avarice or the will to largesse
The will to scepticism or the will to belief
The will to kindness of the will to cruelty
The will to laughter or the will to grief
The will to creativity or the will to sterility
The will to justice or the will to oppression
The will to pride or the will to humility
The will to civility or the will to churlishness
The will to enslavement or the will to freedom
The will to darkness of the will to light
The will to reconciliation of the will to fight
The will to happiness of the will to despair
The will to heaven or the will to hell
The will to be greedy or the will to share
The will to humanity or the will to callousness
The will to conservation or the will to nature's destruction
The will to silence or the will to speak the truth
The will to integrity or the will to depravity

Nothing good happens but is willed by someone
Nothing evil happens but it's willed by someone

But everything is integral, everything is perfect
And the world is a paradise if we do God's will

Then we're *shalom*, just, at peace with ourselves,
God, our fellows, and every creature on the earth;

When the old man finished his final wisdom speech,
He lay down, and drifted softly into an eternal sleep.

A Fat Man's Heaven

Tell me about heaven's halls,
I implored the dead old man,
Since you have seen them all.
I can only tell you in a song he said;
Well then sing on my muse I replied:
He did so and as his song echoed like
A gong in my soul, thus he held forth:

Beside the sea of silence
I saw a secret golden door,
And every greed and violence,
Dissolved inside that door,
For it opened into forever more.

And angels there
Had golden wings,
And soared beyond the pain
Of earthly chains;
And thrones were there
For poets and saintly kings;
And around them
Happy spirits were singing.

And as I entered
Someone said stop!
You forgot your wings.
I am a poet I said,
And that is all
The wings I need.

And I cried, I demand
To be placed in the special place
Reserved for the poets and the kings.

So you shall, St Peter said,
I'll give you the wings of words,
And the harp of rhythmic songs,
To heal your soul of worldly wrongs.

Ah, I said, I see then
This will be a heaven
That will be worthwhile.
And you shall be given
A golden throne, Peter added,
For you wrote to praise God,
And no vain idols of man;
You did not trust only in football teams,
Politicians, or worldly crowns; you knew
They would all let you down in the end;

The Lord won't, though we may let him down,
But because you kept the faith,
And did your best despite your many faults,
And picked yourself up and dusted
Yourself off when you fell,
I'll give you a grand mansion
Among the highly blessed,
Where great music and poetry
Are celebrated day and night,
And light penetrates
The heart to the core,
And sin and sorrow is no more,
Beyond the golden door,
That leads to heaven's jewelled floor.

I am a prophetic poet, I said
And that's bliss
More than I deserve at last.
For to serve the lord,

And express all that's best,
And kind and free and whole,
I knew would gain me a great reward,
Among the eternal revelling saints of the lord.

So, having fitted on my halo,
Said my prayer piece,
Donned my golden wings,
And taken my poetic harp,
And strummed a few lively Irish tunes,
Peter led me without further ado into the great final feast.

Ah, you are codding me,
I said to the dead old man,
You never tasted the grand banquet;
Ha! My poor wan poetic boy, he replied:
So why have I, since you first saw me laid out,
In a short time become gorgeously sleek and fat?

Love and the Unloved

Why is loving people
So frightening
The old man said,
After he'd sobered up,
And drank some coffee,
After a night indulging
In good beer and whiskey.

Maybe because we're afraid
We won't be loved back,
I hazarded a guess, and added
The fear of not being loved
Is the great fear in every human heart,
People can live without many things,
But no one can really live without love.

Here a tear coursed down
The old man's dead face,
For he had a tender heart
As he thought of all
The unloved children and adults
In the world of the fall, living alone
Or on the streets in cardboard boxes,
Their souls shrivelled and gored
By lack of a loving home
Or love of any kind at all.

But we have one consolation
Surely, I cried,
In the special love of God
For his unloved children on earth.
But that is not enough he said,
We must feel his love through others.

And when we have that
We need little else, for
The knowledge of being truly loved
Is our greatest treasure trove.
It should make us dance for joy,
All the day and all the night,
Or burst into tears of delight.

And returning the love,
Let us hold the other so close
That we almost crush them.
People need *to know* they're loved.
For instinctively we're aware
That everything else passes away;
Like the light fading in western fire.
Even amid the pain of illness and death
Love is an silver star of heavenly wealth.

Letting us dream again,
And letting life be a warm cabin,
Summer, autumn of winter;
For the life of love within
Never dies, it always exists
And blooms like a tender kiss
In the blue of everlasting skies.

I wiped away the tears
From the old man's eyes,
The tears he shed
For all the unloved of the earth.
For I loved him,
And despite his faults,
I had been warmed
By the fire of his loving art.
My life was set aglow by his loving heart.

Don't be afraid to cry,
I said, at all the world's lack of love!
For when we cry,
The tears like a sea,
Will wash all our pain away cleanse us inside,
And prove our own hearts at least aren't dead.

Cry on! I said, and love on regardless
Of the coldness of people and the earth
In which we live. Cry on! For the dearth
Of love and hope on every hand,
And bring your love to change all that,
In whatever small way you can.
And then you will prove yourself
To be a living soul, shriven, whole,
Hearty, fit for heaven's kindly shore.

The Old Man Tells of the Heaven of Desire

There is an island
Way out at sea:
Its shores are golden sands,
Its fields stretch to eternity.
It is the heart and soul land
Where we long to be,
Beyond life's turbulent sea.

There are grand unspoiled beaches,
And birds singing in fruit-filled leafy trees:
There are coral reefs of the soul's deep desires;
There are poets constantly composing
Grand symbolic and symphonic songs;
There is a cove into which sail various coloured sails;
There is a well, crystal clear of an island saint of yore.
There is a silhouette of heaven in polished marble stone.

There is a bell tower with a silver door,
That call all to prayer,
In the daily cycle of the hours:
There are turf fires;
And piebald horse herds;
And Connemara pony corrals;
And fiddles playing age-old dance tunes
As of the world's lost delights;
And fair maidens playing harps,
And singing age-old songs of joy.

There all are long white-robed saints:
And couples holding hands under spreading ancient oaks;
There artists paint amazing mural of every wall;
And orchestras play powerful symphonies

Of Bach and Beethoven and Ravel,
In mansions filled with gentlemen and ladies dancing;
There are pretty innocent children playing –
Little auburn curled girls and raven-haired sturdy boys -
Like toys of finest men and women from the glens of yore.

For this is the island of bliss divine
Without disease or war or cruel crime:
No serial killers or gulag-fillers here,
Only fair integral men and women,
And children around crystal wells
Of water pure and clear;
No smoke stacks but air as fresh
As the children wishes;
And each soul and mind free of care.
Here wild hares and foxes play in the heather,
And plover and wild geese shriek
In neat triangles of flight overhead.
Here voices are understood before even said;
And masses of wild animals and birds
Saved from extinction clamour around rocks,
And fruit-laden trees and humming-bee heather.
Here the weather is ever calm and serene:
Seas do not rage but calmly lap onto the golden shores;
And wild herbs – rosemary and sage and bay-leaf trees -
Make sweet the stews and roasts of meat
That adorn the tables of rich and poor alike.
This is the world we would like to attain,
But cannot until perhaps the heaven of the last day.

I cried out, somehow let it be now,
But an angel came and stood by me, the old man said
Do not cry, smile, this is the isle of future design,
After the apocalypse, the restoration of Eden

In the garden of eternal blessedness,
That all attain after a life of goodness.
At this smiles wreathed the old man's face,
And I knew he was already living in wild beautiful
Folds round a home fitted for his gentle godly soul.

In Praise of Youth

There is truth in youth,
The old man said:
Every little girl and boy
Of shining hair and shining eye
Is a wonder, a pearl of great price,
A Jewel of the Lord's design;
Each is unique and new,
And fresh as pine forests,
Scented in pearly morning dew.

There is grace in youth:
Every little shoot, boy or girl
Is ready to be a flower,
Is already a flower of light;
We praise the beauty of nature
But in each youth
There is a finer creation,
A free soul of joy and truth.

They know that grey work
Is not to be, *to play is to be:*
To be free from the logic
Of man, the controlling mentality;
To play freely and imaginatively
Is really to be of the divinity,
From which they lately came.

There is beauty in youth:
Praise it and let it play
Freely in the light;
All they want is love;
Us to say how special
And beautiful each is;

Then they will never grow old,
Or hard like some adults are
In the world, or numb in soul.

There is a future new society
In youth, a breath of fresh air
In our stifling room of care;
The future is in their hands;
Let them shape it freely
In brighter and greener lands.

There is innocence in youth.
At this I broke into his musing
To remind him that youth
Is also part of the fall,
Of the evil one and our first parents.
I know the young can be cruel
To those weaker than themselves,
Cruel in their games,
Calling each other names,
Shutting someone out from their play.
When I was young in school
We fought each other
Like cats and dogs every day;
And yet under it all we were
Innocent as the fields and bogs
Out of which we came.

True the old man said,
Gently nodding his head.
But these times are stranger
Than our poor yet innocent times;
Yet though born into a fallen world,
The youth today too are often close
To the heaven from which they came.

They may drift away from it sadly
As they grow up and learn hard ways;
And forget the glories
Of their youth,
And the pearl of innocence,
And grace and truth,
Given them by the lord of youth.

But they never wholly forget
The womb of innocence
From which they came,
And the lord from which
They received their glory.
Youth I name you:
Megan the marvellous;
Clodagh the golden;
Sarah the amazing;
Luke the evangelist;
Tara the princess;
Leone the lion; Lucy the lovely;
Evan the almighty;
My grand nephews and nieces,
Shining like gold in Kildinan.
Running wild as fawns in the fields;
Young and strong and free,
Before the world grows old beneath
Their flying feet!

Dedication: to Dan and Mairead, May 2022

"Gather ye rosebuds while you may" - Herrick

Lay down my loves
Upon the ground,
And laugh your life away.
Let there be no tears
For you and I,
Among the flowers of May.
The world has enough
Sorrows of its own,
Without creating more
To weigh us down.
Laugh at pain,
And laugh harsh life away,
Like the flowers of May do,
Dancing in showers of hail.
Set aside all gloom,
And bloom while young,
And play without care,
Like the flowers of May do,
Even when covered with coats
Of cruel late-spring snow.

Lay down dear loves,
In a wild flower field,
Of masses of grass, become hay.
Let there be kisses for each other,
My Adam and Eve,
Among the fields of Hay,
And weave the wild flowers
Into crowns, to make you
Kings and queens of May;

Before your youth
Has passed away, and you,
Dear gentleman and lady youth,
Like me, poor poet, have
Grown old and stooped and grey,
Like yesterday's faded flowers of May.

Yet may I too not laugh life away,
For every time is a time of youth,
If we are free from death within,
We stay forever as flowers of May.

Vision of the Bones

Old now, I seem to hear distantly
The tolling of insistent bells,
Calling me slowly and solemnly
To my place in heaven or hell.

And I seemed to see before me
A shining and depthless well, and within
Two angels saying: "leap into the void
And sink to my heaven, or my hell".

One angel's face was bright and happy;
The other's face was dark and cold.
And a voice from the well within me said
Your future fate hinges on which you choose.

And I saw on the cold clay
A great collection of bones,
Crying out to live, for their sins
To be fully and finally atoned.

And amid the collection of bones,
A small collection was mine,
Calling out to me, you will be
Me presently, bones and ashes in clay!

Dying to rise and climb to the heaven,
Or sink like a stone to the hell shaped in the soul.
For great weights were around some bones,
The various leaden weights of unrepentant sins.

These were prevented them from rising
Or being ever free again; but the bones cried out,
And were freed from all bonds of sin by the prayers
Of the church, and the power of Christ's tears of care.

For golden masses were said for them
In the communion of the living
And the dead, the lord's church family
Both in and above the prison of human time.

And like the dry bones in the bible,
My bones thus came to life and sang,
The song of the lord, with a voice free
Of worldly ideologies and free from worldly infamy.

And a voice said, such lives embody useless vanity.
They pass fast to dust's dark well of death every day.
But the bones of the saints stay alive, waiting to put on
Gloriously on the last day, flesh that'll never fade away.

How Literature Works

Like great white lilies
It spurts up,
Out of the sword of light,
As if the body would burst
From desire of her piercing
In the intense night.
What lilies it hurts
With new spasms of blood in life.

This is the knife
That pierces home to the bone.
That leaves us singing in the stone
Of the aortic core,
Ringing in every portal pore;
White glinting butterfly
Of glazed fire,
I burn upwards,
I break loose,
To become a church spire.

II

Art is a slave-driver:
Never satisfied
With what you produce;
Out of your suffering
It produces a pearl,
Yet casts it aside,
Saying it must be
Without price.
Art is a hunger in the blood,
A disease.
It bleeds you dry,
And yet what you leave behind
Is your peace?
The only equivalent
Is to be a priest.

Epilogue

Nothing is ever the same.
The fiery wheel of time
Turns again and again;
All is flux and change.
Yet though time is Lord
Of the world I once knew and loved,
And nothing now seems the same,
I dream and know that in lime-white mansions
Beyond time is written my immortal name.

For though all is flux and change,
The poet writes of timeless truths,
Of nature, life, youth, the heart, and God's art,
The hidden designs of the soul;
These are always ageless and make humankind whole.
These will always bring humankind in from the cold.
That is why I claim that on walls of lime-white mansions
Beyond time and the times is written my immortal name.

The Final Design

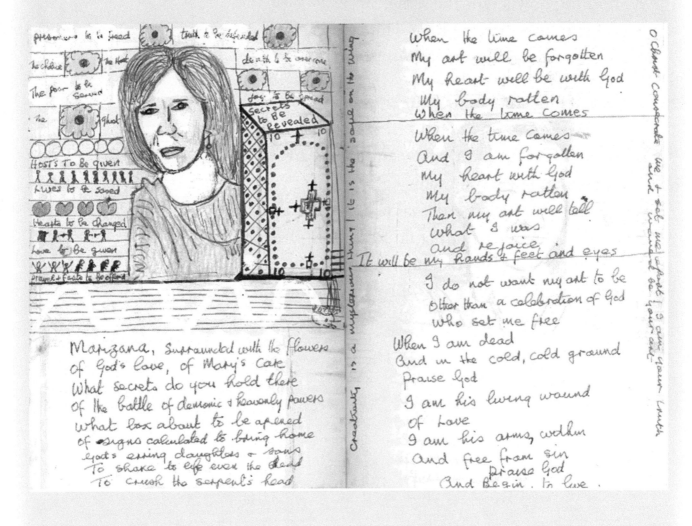

Left page (drawing with handwritten notes):

prisoners to be freed   truth to be defended

to choose   the Host

The poor to be served

the   ghost   death to be overcome

joy to be spread

Secrets to Be Revealed

Hosts To Be given

Lives to be saved

Hearts to be changed

Love to be given

prayers + fasts to be offered

10   10   10

Marizana, Surrounded with the flowers
of God's love, of Mary's Care
What secrets do you hold there
Of the battle of demonic & heavenly powers
what box about to be opened
of signs calculated to bring home
Gods erring daughters & sons
To shake to life even the dead
To crush the serpent's head

Vertical text (left of right page):

Creativity is a mysterious thing / It is the same on the living

Right page:

When the time comes
My art will be forgotten
My heart will be with God
My body rotten
When the time comes

When the time comes
And I am forgotten
My heart with God
My body rotten
Then my art will tell
What I was
And rejoice
It will be my hands & feet and eyes

I do not want my art to be
Other than a celebration of God
Who set me free

When I am dead
And in the cold, cold ground
Praise God
I am his living wound
Of Love
I am his arms within
And free from sin
Praise God
And Begin. to live.

Vertical text (right margin):

O Christ Consoler we + set me free / I am your truth and wound be your art

Acknowledgements

The poet wants to acknowledge those who helped him in this mammoth work. Notably his family, especially Daniel Buckley and Mairead O'Donoghue. Also he thanks Pat Culhane, Noel Murphy, Pat Bonar and Bernard O'Donoghue who have been so supportive. The illustrations of the Ostrich, the Wren and the blackbird are from a collection of bird drawings the poet commissioned from Holly Delaney; he thanks her for her thoughtful work. He also thanks Jean O'Brien who helped in the editing of his previous work. He owes so much to so many people it would be impossible to list them all so if he hasn't mentioned others who helped bring this volume to be as a child of the heart, he begs to be excused.